The Spirit of
CARDINAL BERNARDIN

by
A. E. P. Wall

THE THOMAS MORE PRESS
Chicago, Illinois

Introduction

NOT everyone is fortunate enough to live among heroes. I've been blessed by serving under two heroic publishers, both distinguished churchmen because of their personal spirituality and their leadership qualities. One of them, Joseph Cardinal Bernardin, is the subject of this book. This is not a biography, but an examination of Cardinal Bernardin's thinking and how he came to have the sort of creative mind he has.

Another heroic publisher I came to know well is Lawrence Cardinal Shehan, retired Archbishop of Baltimore, who lent his name at Confirmation to my son, John Wright Wall. John's baptismal name was suggested by another of my personal heroes, John Cardinal Wright, who was prefect of the Sacred Congregation for the Clergy at the time of his death. I never worked for him, although he offered me the editorship of the *Pittsburgh Catholic* when John Deedy left that job to become managing editor of *Commonweal*.

Cardinal Wright, then the Bishop of Pittsburgh, was hailed as a liberal in matters of Church and the plight of the needy before the Second Vatican Council convened. Later he was hailed, by others, as a conservative in matters of religion, although he remained a social liberal.

In reviewing one of his books I once wrote that when friends asked me what had happened to Cardinal Wright, I replied that nothing had happened. His views in 1970 were about the same as his views in 1960; others had changed but he had not. He told me that my observation was right on target.

3

When it seemed to me that one of my personal heroes might become the Archbishop of Chicago (after all, I'd been right about Harry S. Truman in 1948) I read all of the homilies, speeches and articles by Joseph L. Bernardin that I could track down. I gathered several pounds of them, sifted through them and when it turned out that he was the Pope's choice to succeed John Cardinal Cody I was ready.

I wrote a long article for *The Chicago Catholic* explaining the Bernardin outlook on many issues. That article eventually suggested this book, which is not a work of literature but may at least be the world's longest article.

I've found it great to be a spouse, but it has its handicaps. My wife's only handicap is her husband, who for years has taken manuscripts and galley proofs home from work and solicited her advice. I'm especially grateful to Sally for her careful reading of the manuscript for this book.

Our younger son David, who's at ease in the mysterious world of computers and is capable in both math and writing, taught me how to use the IBM word processor. That's a family skill that began with son John, who is talented in handling words and a camera. Daughter Marie and her husband Mark Veldman encouraged me between their exams and long periods of study. After they're both doctors they may find time to read the book. I'm grateful to my mother for helping me to learn how to read before I mastered the tricycle and for brightening my childhood with books. This one is for her.

Valued help has come from many friends, among them Robert B. Beusse, consultant and former secretary of communication for the United States Catholic Conference; Dan Herr, chairman of the board of the Thomas More

Association, who encouraged me to begin this project; Daniel Kane, communication director for the Archdiocese of Cincinnati; Rev. John R. Keating, Chancellor, Vicar General and former Administrator of the Archdiocese of Chicago (now Bishop of Arlington, VA.); Archbishop Thomas P. Kelly, O.P., of Louisville; Dolores Madlener, my administrative secretary; Sal Miragliotta, National Catholic News Service librarian; Octavie Mosimann, Cardinal Bernardin's long-time secretary; and Rev. James P. Roache, the Cardinal's administrative assistant.

Cardinal Bernardin has read the manuscript and pointed out errors—any remaining errors are mine—but he has made no effort to influence the content of the book. His patience and consideration are limitless.

A.E.P. Wall

Chapter One

YOU didn't have to live in Chicagoland, as the sprawling metropolitan area that includes the nation's second largest city is known, to join in the guessing game. Almost everybody had a name to drop into the conversation whenever talk turned to a new Archbishop for Chicago.

Reporters phoned from Buffalo, St. Paul, Baltimore, Miami, New York, Washington; it seemed as though they called from any city that had a telephone. They had rumors to check and wanted to talk with anybody on the staff of *The Chicago Catholic*, the archdiocesan weekly newspaper. They were looking for confirmation, for a strong clue that their candidate would succeed the controversial John Cardinal Cody.

Denials make poor headlines, and a country almost saturated with radio newscasts, television news extravaganzas and a newspaper on every doorstep wants facts but will settle for the titilation of colorful guessing.

Everybody had expected that Cardinal Cody would retire on his 75th birthday, because that's the way the regulations read and Cardinal Cody was a stickler for the formalities of the Catholic Church. After all, Cardinal Cody was immersed in newspaper clippings and television transcripts of stories about his financial dealings and personal relationships. It was a scandal that caught the elderly Archbishop of Chicago by surprise.

His denial of the accusations was not enough to satisfy most of his followers or most of the media. Specific denial, point by point, was demanded by almost everyone. At first the Cardinal was anxious to respond. Work began on a lengthy document of denial, item by item, but the Cardinal hesitated. Would there be more accusations before he could complete his elaborate denial? He decided to wait. He told friends that his lawyers didn't want him to make any detailed denials. He said that he'd follow that advice and stand by his general denial that he'd done anything wrong. After retirement, he told one associate, he would go into all of the issues in his memoirs.

He did not retire and settle in at St. Mary of the Lake Seminary to work quietly on those memoirs. He apparently died at home before an ambulance whisked him to Northwestern Memorial Hospital, just down the street from his office. He was pronounced dead at 12:19 a.m. April 29, 1982.

A tired journalistic phrase, often overworked, was entirely apt: It was the end of an era in Chicago and in much of the Catholic Church. Cardinal Cody was the product of an earlier time. "I often yearn," he once said with a half smile, "for the old days when I could issue an edict and know that my will would be carried out."

Cardinal Cody's troubles inevitably became troubles for the Catholic Church, for Catholics in Chicago and everywhere. The *New York Times*, national television networks, the Associated Press, dailies in London and Dublin, weeklies in Toronto and Singapore delivered the story wherever English is understood. It was a story that demanded translation, because scandal has a universal appeal. It was a story talked about over cups of espresso and glasses of Campari inside Vatican City.

Who could ever set things straight in the largest archdiocese in the United States, home of two-and-a-half million Catholics, workplace for some of the country's exemplary specialists in canon law, theology, Scripture, liturgy, Catholic social action and almost any other subject listed in the *Catholic Almanac's* table of contents.

A series of stories that began in the *Chicago Sun-Times* reached out to the whole Christian world and to a substantial segment of the rest of the world.

Chicago's troubles began years before the *Sun-Times* began to look into Cardinal Cody's personal and financial life, long before a federal grand jury began an investigation that ended with the Cardinal's death. Sparring between some of his priests and the outspoken Archbishop of Chicago was known to newspaper readers for years.

When Pope John Paul II visited Chicago in 1979 he saw posters, written in Polish, protesting Cardinal Cody's decision to close the city's Sacred Heart Shrine. Before he left Vatican City he knew that complaining letters had reached there over a period of years, many of them written by priests and sisters.

Cardinal Cody's supporters, who were numerous, were less outspoken than his critics. They published fewer newsletters, gave fewer speeches, lettered fewer signs, walked in fewer protest lines. They shared the Cardinal's calm assurance that he was right and that nothing else mattered. After all, a Chicago Cardinal was untouchable. And it was a fact that Cardinal Cody had carried out all sorts of mandates and suggestions that came out of the Second Vatican Council.

The Archdiocese of Chicago was ahead of most of the world in creating new offices and agencies to meet the special needs of the divorced, the Spanish-speaking immigrants living in an unfamiliar U.S. society, the members of the Charismatic movement and the handicapped.

Chicago had a Clergy Personnel Board, an Office of Communications, a Catholic Family Consultation Service, an Office of Conciliation and Arbitration, a Cursillo Movement, and an Archdiocesan Office for Development, an Archdiocesan Office for Goal Setting and another office for Health Affairs, an Office for the Laity and an Office for Parish Councils. It had an Office for the Ministry of Peace and Justice.

It had the largest number of permanent deacons in the country and its own Catholic Television Network of Chicago. Ethnics? There were archdiocesan centers for Chinese, Haitians, Italians, Koreans, Lithuanians and Vietnamese. Cardinal Cody boasted that the liturgy was celebrated regularly in sixteen languages within his Archdiocese of Chicago.

His Archdiocese of Chicago? He sometimes spoke of it as his, and that led to some confrontations. Under Illinois law he was the corporation sole, the holder in trust of a couple of billion dollars in real estate and other church property. "I own it," he said more than once while regarding a school or church building under his control.

How he exercised that trust was the question raised by the grand jury and the *Sun-Times*, answered broadly by a Cardinal Cody who denied any misuse of trust but never answered point by point, as the Cardinal insisted he would do after his retirement.

Years before his death closed the official investigation there was speculation that a private Vatican study, responding to letters sent to the Pope and the Pope's representative to the United States hierarchy, the Apostolic Delegate in Washington, had Cardinal Cody on the defensive.

The Cardinal scoffed at this, but he knew that powerful figures in the Church thought it was time for him to retire long before he reached the mandatory 75. If he won't retire, those figures argued, he should be given a coadjutor archbishop with the authority to make decisions. Cardinal Cody knew what that meant. He'd been named the coadjutor with right of succession to Bishop Charles H. LeBlond of St. Joseph, Mo., in 1954; in 1956 he'd been made coadjutor with right of succession to Archbishop Edwin V. O'Hara of Kansas City-St. Joseph. Finally, in 1961 he had been appointed coadjutor with right of succession to Archbishop Joseph Rummel of New Orleans. He did not want a coadjutor archbishop in Chicago, but he had an idea who would be named if that should come to pass.

He told friends that if he should be nudged into retirement ahead of time he would "tell all" in a book he planned to write, but never had to write. Just as the speculation, and the Cardinal's concern, reached a new peak there was tragedy in Rome. Pope Paul VI died. It was during the latter part of his pontificate, as complaints and criticisms mounted, that speculation about the future of Chicago's Cardinal grew.

One of Pope Paul's curial officials, Sebastiano Cardinal Baggio, visited Chicago for private conversations with Cardinal Cody, then went on to Latin America. Cardinal Baggio, the head of the Vatican Congregation for Bishops, returned to Rome from Latin America for the funeral of Paul VI. His Chicago report would be moot. It is doubtful whether the Holy See's pursuit of the truth in the turbulent Chicago situation will ever be released from the Vatican archives. Whether Pope Paul VI ever made a decision will probably never be verified.

But the public pressure continued. Some said that the publicity gained by Cardinal Cody's opponents worked against them. The Holy See, it was said, was unlikely to give the appearance of yielding to the pressure of press releases. Cardinal Cody and his supporters felt vindicated when the complaints, which were known to the Cardinal, apparently went unanswered.

But Cardinal Cody knew that his position had been shaken, his authority diminished. He continued to insist that his way was correct, that his good intentions were being subverted by critics who did not understand him or who sought recognition for themselves at his expense. In Chicago you can still get an argument on either side of that question.

Nobody, not even Cardinal Cody, underestimated the gravity of the troubles in Chicago. It would take a man of heroic spirituality and administrative genius to sort out the troubles, even to identify all of them accurately and then to overcome them.

Chapter Two

"CHICAGOLAND Catholics reached out to embrace their new archbishop. To their delight, he hugged back." That's how I began the news account of Archbishop Joseph L. Bernardin's arrival to take over the spiritual and temporal government of the Catholic Church of Chicago.

Chicagoland had never welcomed a new resident with so much enthusiasm. The newspapers nudged each other with bigger and more colorful pictures, warmer and more appreciative stories. Television crews recorded and edited miles of taped images of the new Archbishop. Radio stations tried to beat each other on the air with the latest word on what Archbishop Bernardin said, ate, read, thought; where he walked, how he walked, where he stood, when his furniture would arrive, where his plane would land.

The *Sun-Times*, its disapproval of the late Cardinal Cody shoved past the classified pages and out of the paper, lit up its front page like a Technicolor billboard. The *Tribune*, having discarded its famous slogan, somehow managed to behave as though it were the "world's greatest newspaper" reporting on the world's greatest archbishop.

Television crews commuted between Chicago and Cincinnati, crowding into a press conference at the Cathedral of St. Peter in Chains, where Archbishop Bernardin had been installed a decade before, photographing the outside of the rectory at St. Louis Church in downtown Cincinnati, where Archbishop Bernardin occupied a pleasant but modest apartment.

The Pope's announcement caught some archbishop-watchers by surprise. Millions were waiting for word about who would take over the troubled affairs left behind by a tired and ailing John Cardinal Cody. For years the energetic Archbishop of Cincinnati had been a front-runner in almost everybody's predictions, but other names cropped up.

Some thought his chances of coming to Chicago had been damaged by a magazine article suggesting that the internationally-known priest-author Andrew Greeley had tried to advance the Bernardin cause, although those who knew Archbishop Bernardin and those who knew how the Holy See functions paid only passing attention to the article. Father Greeley denied the article's implications, saying that the piece was based on fantasy.

The suggestion was so out of character for Archbishop Bernardin that it was instantly rejected by his friends. His friends included Pope John Paul II. Even Cardinal Cody expected that the vigorous Archbishop of Cincinnati, who had proven himself in one responsible post after another, would succeed him.

The appointment was personal, based on shared experiences and respect. It began with an invitation from the Pope. Would Archbishop Bernardin call on him in Vatican City? The Archbishop would. He set off for Rome with an old Cincinnati friend, Father Alvin T. Zugelter.

They checked in at Rome's Holiday Inn, where they were able to take advantage of a clergy discount and, incidentally, to confound reporters and others of inquiring disposition who tried to reach him at Villa Stritch, where many American prelates spend their time in Rome, or at one of the premier hotels of the city. No reason had been given for the invitation to Rome. Archbishop Bernardin had a hunch, but he knew nothing for certain.

The Cincinnati visitors headed for Vatican City, where Father Zugelter occupied himself in an outer room while Archbishop Bernardin was received by a man who, as the Archbishop of Cracow, had visited him in Cincinnati during a 1976 tour of much of the United States. A reminder of that visit, a glistening crystal vase presented by the Polish visitor, stood on a table in Archbishop Bernardin's Cincinnati apartment.

For half an hour Pope John Paul and Archbishop Bernardin talked about Chicagoland and the Catholic Church. The Pope already knew Chicago intimately, perhaps better than he knew any other American city. He had included Chicago in his 1976 tour, toasted by the late Mayor Richard J. Daley, Cardinal Cody, his close friend Auxiliary Bishop Alfred L. Abramowicz and thousands of others. He probably remembered the sign calling upon him in Polish to help Sacred Heart supporters to "Save Our Shrine" from Cardinal Cody's decision to shut it down.

During that conversation in one of the venerable rooms in the Vatican, where many events in world history have been initiated or given a nudge, Pope John Paul II asked Archbishop Bernardin to accept the Chicago appointment. The answer quickly became part of the history of the Catholic Church in the United States and its ripples began gently rocking world events. It also became, instantly, one of the major religious news stories of the year. It was time to end the speculation and calm the rumors.

While most Catholics in Chicago and Cincinnati were still in bed the sun was shining in Rome, where the announcement was made official on Saturday, the tenth of July, 1982. For Archbishop Bernardin it was a time for prayers of dedication to his new assignment and thanksgiving for what he saw as God's calling him to stretch his abilities to the limit. The news was out. There was time to check out of the Holiday Inn, to relax with a Campari and soda and to drive familiar streets and highways to Rome's Leonardo da Vinci Airport at Fiumicino.

Archbishop Bernardin and Father Zugelter were not prepared for the size of the news corps that was standing by at the airport when they made it home, radiant but pursued by the relentless jet lag that saps the energy of travelers crossing one time zone after another. The jet lag didn't show; the radiance did. Reporters were greeted as valued friends. Words were recorded in notebooks and on television film.

Finally, at home in his rooms diagonally across the street from the building that houses principal offices of the Archdiocese of Cincinnati, Archbishop Bernardin settled in with the telephone.

He wanted to talk with Father John R. Keating, known as Dick to his special friends and as the interim administrator of the Archdiocese of Chicago to millions. Father Keating, chancellor of the Archdiocese, vicar general and a member of the Board of Consultors, had been elected to run things until Cardinal Cody's successor could be named. My phone at home rang. It was Archbishop Bernardin calling from Cincinnati. He listened patiently to my congratulations, but what he really wanted was Father Keating's home phone number. He finally reached Father Keating early Sunday, solidifying a feeling of shared respect. He spoke also with Bishop Nevin W. Hayes, O.Carm., and Bishop Abramowicz, Chicago's two auxiliaries, both old friends of the new Archbishop of Chicago.

That Sunday was muggy in Cincinnati, that hospitable city on the Ohio River, across from Covington, Ky. Reporters prowled the streets, visited churches, talked with strollers. Sisters carrying books from a shop next to the St. Louis rectory entrance on sunny, steaming Eighth Street, looked up to see a photographer recording their steps.

The Archbishop relaxed at home, his first chance to settle back after extraordinarily active days. He'd had very little sleep during the previous twenty-four hours. He had supper with Father Zugelter, pastor of St. Louis Church and in that sense the Archbishop's landlord; Father Thomas C. Nolker, the Archbishop's youthful-looking administrative assistant; Daniel Kane, director of the Archbishop's Office of Communications, and a visitor from Chicago who remembered the events well enough to record them here.

Archbishop Bernardin took a quick look at the Chicago Sunday newspapers while everyone relaxed in shirt-sleeves. After the fresh fruit and cheese were cleared away Archbishop Bernardin took an elevator up one flight from Father Zugelter's floor to his apartment, which included a small study and a living room designed for relaxation. There he phoned Archbishop Pio Laghi, the Apostolic Delegate in Washington, and Father Keating to work out the date for his installation. It was then mid-July; the installation would be August 25, the Feast of St. Louis, in Chicago's Holy Name Cathedral.

Archbishop Bernardin officially took possession the night before the installation, when he presented his credentials to the Consultors at the cathedral while his brother priests looked on. It was formalized in a grand liturgical way on August 25 when Holy Name vibrated with voices, organs, bells and brass. Ten cardinals, more than 20 archbishops, more than 100 bishops, interfaith leaders, Governor James Thompson of Illinois and Mayor Jane Byrne of Chicago and all the invited guests the cherished old cathedral could hold were there for the solemn liturgy of installation.

For many it was a joyous return to Holy Name Cathedral, where just four months earlier they had gathered for the funeral of Cardinal Cody. For the Archbishop's mother, other family members, friends and associates from his days in Columbia and Charleston in his native state of South Carolina, from the time he served as auxiliary bishop in Georgia's capital city of Atlanta, from the years he spent as general secretary of the National Conference of Catholic Bishops and the United States Catholic Conference in Washington, D.C., from his decade in Cincinnati, it was time to show a bit of pride and even a tear without embarrassment.

Chicago had a new Archbishop. It was love at first sight, according to the media. How long would the honeymoon last?

Chapter Three

YOU don't have to celebrate a silver wedding anniversary to know that a honeymoon doesn't have to end. Some love affairs just go on and on, not evenly intense but authentically alive. That's my answer when somebody warns me that Cardinal Bernardin is still enjoying his honeymoon with the media and the public. It looks like a marriage that will last.

It could last for a long time, because if the actuarial tables, statistics and church retirement regulations hold up there will be a Cardinal Bernardin on the job in Chicago at least until April 2, 2003.

Some say he will be Pope before then, a suggestion that exasperates a busy man who has plenty to do. Those suggestions come from Catholics, Protestants, Jews and others who know that Cardinal Bernardin was a member of the World Synod of Bishops long before Chicago thought seriously about having him as a permanent resident, who have felt the strength of his personality, who know that he received the red hat of a Cardinal just five months after he was installed in Chicago. It is not a suggestion that Cardinal Bernardin wants to keep alive.

A couple of years before he died, Cardinal Cody sat with a friend in the reception room of the stately residence which Chicago Catholics have long provided for their archbishops. It was once the "throne room."

Cardinal Cody explained that it once was customary for all cardinals to have a papal chair in their homes in case of a visit from the Pope. There was a search for the throne when it was learned that Pope John Paul II would stay at the residence. It was located in the basement, brightened up with fresh gilt and put in place for the Pope to use.

In that room, which was furnished with red chairs and illuminated by a chandelier decorated with red crystal roses, Cardinal Cody chatted with friends and spoke more severely to the unlucky ones who were called on its thick but subdued carpet. It was in that room that Cardinal Cody remarked that in his opinion the Pope wanted to make Archbishop Bernardin a cardinal and almost certainly would do so.

Regardless of whether he was right at the time, Cardinal Cody's prediction was given swift reality just months after his successor was installed in Holy Name Cathedral and after he moved into the official residence. The red drapes didn't last, and Cardinal Bernardin is likely to receive visitors in his inviting, tastefully decorated study. Unlike Cardinal Cody, who did most of his office work at home, Cardinal Bernardin works long hours in his downtown office. He plans his time carefully because there's never enough of it.

Even before he became chairman of the committee of United States bishops given the massive job of drafting a pastoral letter on the moral dimensions of war and peace, Cardinal Bernardin was known to much of the world. Invitations to speak, requests for interviews, ideas for articles and pleas for appointments are almost overwhelming.

Whether his picture is on the cover of *Time* magazine or *The New York Times Magazine*, whether he's interviewed on the *Today* show or nationally televised during a news conference, he's in millions of minds day by day. Many want to help him; many want him to help them.

What sort of a man is it who can attract the affections of

so many, give courage to so many, inspire so many to try to improve the spiritual foundations of their lives? What kind of person can write so well, read so widely, interpret so broadly, preach so effectively, lead so energetically, address himself to so many topics so thoroughly?

Italian Americans embrace Cardinal Bernardin as a member of the family, and he responds with gestures of joy. At one festive Italian-American event in Chicago the Cardinal grinned at the camera and quipped, "Eat your hearts out, all you Poles and Irish!" That was part of the party spirit, a time to be happy, but with it all a recognition that because he's an American and his major constituency is American he can wisecrack without being misunderstood, giving offense or even being taken too seriously.

Cardinal Bernardin enjoys his Italian heritage, but not in quite the way that his friend the Pope enjoys his Polish heritage. That's because John Paul II was born a Pole while Cardinal Bernardin was born an American, and a South Carolina American at that. All South Carolinians insist that there's something special about that. It is not possible to understand this complex man if he is not understood to be an American who wants, as many Americans want, to identify in a fruitful way with the rest of the world.

Cardinal Bernardin is not an Italian churchman. He does not react to events the way Italian bishops react to them and he cannot, because in Italy he is a visitor with strong family ties, but nevertheless a visitor. If he had been born in London rather than Columbia he might be known today as Sir Joseph or Lord Bernardin rather than as His Eminence the Cardinal. His sense of dignity is more European than Rotarian despite his constant reaching out to people. He beholds the same dignity in others, even when they don't recognize it in themselves.

Cardinal Bernardin, the man of dignity, strolled along the aisles of the TWA plane that flew him and members of his party home from the Vatican Consistory that gave him his red hat. His coat was left behind at his seat. He was smiling, casual, greeting all of the passengers and stepping aside politely when a flight attendant told him that she needed to clear the aisles long enough to whip away the remains of dinner.

He tries to put others at ease and sometimes that means he must look at ease. He is a man of deep sensibilities, not always openly emotional but always aware of moods and atmospheres. Those who work most closely with him sometimes suspect that he knows what they're thinking, a state of affairs that has the advantage of keeping the thinking on course.

Nobody can really understand Cardinal Bernardin who does not grasp the reality that his is a revealed religion, a Christianity as available to his mother as to a Scripture scholar, as much at hand to a typist as to the author of a theological gem, as open to the embrace of a child falling asleep as to a famous homilist in the pulpit. He *experiences* God while many talk about God, read about God or write about God. This revealed religion is central to everything there is to know about Joseph Bernardin. His own life is an illustration of the fact, a fact which he and other fortunates know, that belief concerns the entire person, encompasses everything that the person does.

Sometimes a person watching Cardinal Bernardin presiding at a liturgical event, wearing the robes and other signs of a solemn occasion, may think for a moment that it is pure drama unfolding and that all of the trappings will vanish, disclosing a man who, even without the markings of office, is still the Cardinal, comfortable in the certain presence of God.

There is no hope of understanding Cardinal Bernardin without recognizing his sense of decency, which is fundamental to his character. He is a decent person, eager to locate the decency in everyone and to encourage its presence. This sense of decency is sometimes offered in explanation of his determination to meet others at least half way, to understand other points of view and to talk things over. He consults. He wants to know what others think. He may solicit a couple of dozen comments before he releases an article he's written or a talk he's prepared.

Wide consultation can be a blessing for a teacher, and Cardinal Bernardin seldom stops teaching, but it includes some hazards for an administrator. It invites gossip, suggestions shaded by malice, ideas connected to maneuvering for position. But Cardinal Bernardin sifts it all, savors it, examines it and then makes up his own mind.

What happens after he makes up his mind? How does he pass his thinking along? Does he write his own speeches? What are the influences that reach the head of the most influential see in the United States?

Chapter Four

IT was after a Sunday morning Mass at St. Clement's Church in Chicago, a couple of miles north of the Cardinal's residence and a couple of blocks west of sprawling Lincoln Park. I stopped to thank the pastor, Father John F. Fahey, for his homily, which had done the kind of thing that most good homilies do. It had made me uneasy about my own way of doing things but had encouraged me to emulate the widely-advertised car rental slogan and try harder.

Most of the homilies at St. Clement's are that kind and probably the celebrant hears a lot of comments like mine. Whatever his reason, he changed the subject. He knew that I had gone to Rome with the small group that accompanied Cardinal Bernardin to the Consistory and he had some questions to ask about it.

Then he asked about the Cardinal's talks and articles, already highly valued in Chicago, and about the column the Cardinal writes weekly for *The Chicago Catholic*. Who writes all of that material?

A day or so later I flew to Washington for a meeting of the Liaison Committee that brings members of the Catholic Press Association and the staff of the National Catholic News Service together for two days every year. During lunch in a Thomas Circle hotel that has changed its name about as many times as an old-fashioned Hollywood actress—I've known it as the Sonesta, Ramada, America and International and it was then contemplating another marriage—a priest-editor asked me the same question. Ghost writers are not unknown in the Catholic Church or

24

among government officials in Washington, and some diocesan newspaper editors are delighted to quote themselves when they write a news account of a speech given by the bishop who publishes their newspaper.

Cardinal Bernardin writes much of his material personally, sometimes by longhand and sometimes on a typewriter. He asks many questions before he turns out his final manuscript. He consults about almost everything except, perhaps, what kind of a collar to wear. He sometimes asks respected friends and specialists in various fields to prepare drafts on particular subjects in which they are experts, to take a look at what he's written and to comment on it. He has done more of this since moving to Chicago because there are more talks to give and less time available for preparing them.

He assumes final responsibility for everything that goes into his talks, even when others have assisted him. He sometimes makes use of research, as most good writers do. But a Chicago priest who told me that he knew who wrote Cardinal Bernardin's important address to the Chicago Board of Rabbis and the Jewish Federation of Greater Chicago probably didn't realize that the Cardinal had polished the final words at about 4 o'clock in the morning on the day he was to give the address.

Like other inordinately busy men and women who are invited frequently to speak to many kinds of audiences, Cardinal Bernardin sometimes relies on specialists to help out with drafts, but the final product is his, the result of his own editing, polishing, rewriting. While he was traveling in Poland as president of the National Conference of Catholic Bishops he faced what seemed to observers to be a painful necessity to yield to a specialist who drafted material in English for translation into Polish. He was less

comfortable than usual with material that did not bear his
original imprint and that, in another languge, was not subject to his purposeful choice of words.

Cardinal Bernardin quips that he sometimes "recycles"
his material. What he means is that he sometimes goes
back to earlier addresses and articles to pick up a phrase
here and there, saving himself from repeating his original
research. Sometimes he will use a good talk again, for
a different audience, without many changes. That sort
of thing is a common practice. It is one reason why
newspapers spend large amounts of money on maintaining
their news libraries, which produce no revenue of consequence but which are worth far more than their weight in
clippings and microfilm.

My first awkward moment with the new Archbishop of
Chicago came after we had talked about the idea of
a weekly column to be written by him for the Chicago
archdiocesan newspaper. My potential columnist agreed
to write one, and said he probably would recycle some of
his earlier Cincinnati columns at the outset. In my
eagerness I misunderstood what he meant by recycling and
began what I intended to be a series of reprints from the
Cincinnati columns. After the first one appeared in print I
learned an embarrassing lesson.

Cardinal Bernardin may reach back into things he has
written in the past, choosing an idea or a phrase or a theme
that will launch him into his new writing. Sometimes he
may use an earlier talk or article with few changes, but
even then he reserves the right to update the material or
modify it to meet new circumstances. Checking back into
earlier work offers advantages to the writer. It helps any
writer not simply to reclaim an idea but to avoid repeating
something that has become familiar.

Having written a remarkable number of editorials about Christmas and Easter, I sometimes check back in the files of clippings to make certain that I'm not repeating myself. I've even written an editorial or two about St. Shinran's Day, an important occasion for Buddhists in Hawaii.

For Cardinal Bernardin, recycling no doubt includes some of that—the avoidance of material that has become familiar and the adapting of other material that needs to be restated, reemphasized to address current conditions. This is a talent in itself and it means much to audiences. At one time I was chairman of the Board of Regents at Chaminade University of Honolulu when commencement day dawned, sunny and breezy as usual on Chaminade's hillside campus. The principal address was given by the bishop, a man I admired, but the words seemed familiar. I was certain that I had heard them before, perhaps more than once before. Finally I asked the bishop, who acknowledged with a broad smile of achievement that he had given the same commencement address that he used at all high school ceremonies.

That's not what Cardinal Bernardin means by recycling. His work, which embodies the results of all of that consulting and research, is as much his own as the legendary address scribbled by Abraham Lincoln on the back of an envelope six score years ago was Lincoln's.

Cardinal Bernardin, his new red hat scarcely out of its box, turned to his friend Msgr. Edward Egan of the Roman Rota for some translation consultation before he delivered one message. It was the Italian language version of his homily at his titular church of Jesus the Divine Worker, *Gesu, Divino Lavoratore*. But it was adapted from the English language homily, which was the Cardinal's own.

He used it to reaffirm his conviction that the Spirit
unites all in faith, regardless of where they live or what
tongue they speak. "The Church is a mystery," he said.
"It is a spiritual reality which exists in the world and is
influenced by the world. But it can never be fully understood; its mission cannot be truly appreciated unless we go
beyond the human, visible structures of the Church so that
we can see and experience the power of Jesus and his Holy
Spirit at work." He didn't stop there: "And yet the visible
structures are important. They are the instruments through
which the Spirit continues the mission of Jesus. They provide the framework in which we humans can literally
encounter the Lord and experience his saving grace. They
are the signs of the inner dynamism which gives life and
vitality to the community of believers."

Cardinal Bernardin, conscious of the symbolism in-
voked by the tradition of titular churches in Rome for cardinals serving elsewhere, of its meaning to brotherhood
and sisterhood in a universal Church, went on to say:
"One of these structures, established by Jesus himself, is
the papacy. The Holy Father is Christ's vicar, the visible
head of the Church. He is the visible sign of the Church's
unity."

Cardinal Bernardin relates to the Pope not only as a
respected friend who is admired throughout the world, not
only as a man whose spirituality merits emulation, but
as the vicar of Jesus Christ. This is an authentic Roman
Catholic view and one that is shared by uncounted
millions, because even those who have not known the personal friendship enjoyed by Cardinal Bernardin and John
Paul II think of the pope as a particular friend. That quality, which is called charismatic but which is actually almost
impossible to define, is shared by both men.

Cardinal Bernardin also has countless friends he's never met, although they know him and are inspired by his personal holiness. How many members of your family and how many of your friends can you describe as holy? You may be fortunate in knowing any number of holy men and women; you may bless others by your own holiness. Yet it is a personal quality that is less visible on the freeway or in the shopping mall than it ought to be.

It is perceived almost the way that radiant health is perceived. Personal holiness radiates, like an electric heater in a cold room, and it causes others to rub their hands together in awareness. When it radiates from an archbishop it tends to move people and things, drawing people into prayer, encouraging the young to yield more readily to the impulses that draw them toward vocations of service. Like television transmission waves that enter a room unseen, personal holiness is picked up and made visible by sensitive receivers.

Cardinal Bernardin would probably be impatient with that description. If he were to walk into a doctor's office for a physical examination a waiting nurse might describe him as a slender man, wearing glasses that mark off a high forehead, a man with a neat and traditional haircut and with a face that doesn't stand still. It smiles a lot and it grows intense when the Cardinal asks a question or listens closely to anyone who is speaking to him.

The nurse would note that the smiling, slender man speaks gently and that all of the words come out distinctly. The nurse would be brought into conversation right away, because there are no background people for Cardinal Bernardin. He doesn't see nurses, waiters, parking attendants, secretaries or reporters as part of the scenery. He sees each person as a person and if he can manage it he'll find a way to greet that person, enter into conversation, learn something and share something.

Before I moved to Chicago in 1976 my secretary was Mary Bozzonetti, who has been the major associate of every director of the National Catholic News Service in Washington. She was there when I started and when Bishop Bernardin was general secretary of the National Conference of Catholic Bishops, sharing the same address at 1312 Massachusetts Avenue, N.W. Almost overnight he became Archbishop Bernardin, the ordinary of the Archdiocese of Cincinnati and then president of the Conference. Toward the end of a sunny Washington afternoon a figure dressed in black rushed into the news agency offices, soon rushed out again to head for National Airport. A smiling Mary Bozzonetti walked over to my desk and summed it up: "That man is certainly one of the busiest people in the country, but he never comes into this building without stopping to say hello. I hope that the people of Cincinnati deserve him!"

After he moved to Chicago his schedule became heavier than the mayor's on the day before an election. He received as many as fifteen or twenty invitations to speak on a single day. But a secretary told me that after her husband died she received a warm and bracing note from the Cardinal that changed her whole outlook on the years ahead. "I'm going to have it framed," she said.

A priest mentioned that the Cardinal had been one of the first to appear at his mother's wake, apologizing that a long-standing engagement would prevent him from being at the funeral. A clerical employee who served in an honor guard treasured a letter of appreciation he received from Cardinal Bernardin. One of his first moves as the new

Archbishop of Chicago was an order to rip out the time clocks that employees had punched each morning and evening in the Archdiocesan Administrative Center. And he renamed the place, too. It became the Archdiocesan Pastoral Center. He wanted his employees to see themselves as he did, as co-workers in the pastoral activities of the Church of Jesus Christ.

Soon after that he met with the heads of offices and departments and agencies, many of them located in the Archdiocesan Pastoral Center and others scattered throughout Cook and Lake Counties. He said that he could not carry the whole burden and didn't want to, that he would need abundant help and authentic cooperation. He offered dialogue and consultation, but said that he could not personally meet frequently with fifty or so heads of agencies and offices. Each man and woman there agreed with him and responded to his eagerness to know them and to understand their work.

This was an early signal to his Chicago associates of his skills in getting things done through people, of recognizing individual effort and encouraging it, of presenting formal and tacit guidelines. In South Carolina, where he began his priesthood, in Atlanta where he was an auxiliary bishop, in Washington, where he led the reorganization of the headquarters of the United States hierarchy, in Cincinnati, where he headed a large archdiocese, in Rome, where he was an energetic leader in the World Synod of Bishops—in all of those places and over a long period of time he was known as an exemplary administrator who understood people and relied upon them more than he did on organizational charts.

Chicago quickly found that it had an administrator of

exceptional competence at the head of a Church that had
been drifting during the period of Cardinal Cody's declining health. It had a man who not only liked to write his
own speeches whenever possible, but who seemed to write
his own rules for getting things done. Whether he was
preparing a talk or organizing a department, he did it with
his people in mind.

Chapter Five

WHAT kind of a picture pops into your mind when somebody mentions a bureaucrat? The word is one that's sometimes used derisively, as though all bureaucrats were aimless shufflers of paper trying to fill in the time until the end of another day. But the world turns on a pencil, a spike or a spindle.

The world is full of paper, most of it with things written on it. A good bureaucrat keeps the pencil sharp, the spike cleared at the end of the day and the spindle spinning.

Although the claim has none of the aura of dogma, it may still be a fact that the Catholic Church is the original bureaucracy. If you treasure your Bible it may be possible because some ancient bureaucrat, straining to work by the light of a candle or an oil wick, helped to copy and assemble that treasure for you. The Church is not only the source of a spiritual tradition that enriches millions of 20th Century lives, and the lives of millions who will draw upon that tradition in the 21st Century; it is the source of information, facts by the bookful, pictures by the museumful, traditions that fill the mind and heart.

If it were not for those forgotten bureaucrats of the Church it would be almost impossible to establish the authenticity of Scripture that is taken for granted now. Bureaucrats keep records of births and weddings and ordinations. Modern bureaucrats have traded in their scrolls for word processors, but they still guarantee that what's essential will not be forgotten or lost.

So I was not surprised when Archbishop Thomas C. Kelly, O.P., of Louisville told me that he was greatly interested in the transition of Cardinal Bernardin, "the completion or fulfillment of his bureaucratic abilities, his administrative talents, into service as a full-time shepherd of the largest diocese in the United States."

Archbishop Kelly was aboard the plane that flew friends and family of Cardinal Bernardin to Rome for the red hat Consistory. He was there as a close friend of long standing. The two men had worked together in Washington, where the Dominican Father Tom Kelly became associate general secretary of the National Conference of Catholic Bishops and the United States Catholic Conference in 1971. Before that he was secretary at the Apostolic Delegation in Washington.

As the newly-ordained Bishop Kelly he became general secretary of the Conference and an auxiliary bishop of Washington in 1977, eventually moving a bit further from his hometown of Rochester, N.Y., to historic Louisville. He first met Joe Bernardin in Washington in the late 1960s. He was already, Archbishop Kelly recalled, an accomplished administrator. "He had a great talent for management, for finances, and understood those things," Archbishop Kelly told me during a recent conversation. "Much of that came out of his South Carolina and Georgia experience. When he joined the Conference he had to take on a full new set of responsibilities that called for diplomacy in dealing with the government and the Holy See. He mastered all of that quickly. For someone who had scarcely been out of South Carolina for very long he took to the Washington scene quite well.

"I can't say that he ever liked it there very well. I don't think that one would ever be able to say that his happiest years were in Washington. It is a difficult job being general secretary. You're responsible to far too many people to be able to please them all. If you do the job right it's just inevitable that you're going to make some folks unhappy. But he managed well and as few people as possible got unhappy with Bishop Bernardin."

Archbishop Kelly thinks that Cincinnati made a great difference to its new archbishop. Not long after he arrived there he wrote his first pastoral letter. The theme, not surprising to anyone who knew him well, was prayer. He issued a letter to priests on the same topic. In both of those documents, Archbishop Kelly believes, his friend made a deep commitment to prayer. "I certainly don't want to suggest that he wasn't a prayerful man before, but I believe that those two documents marked a kind of watershed for him. Having articulated his basic understanding of prayer he began to live it out with a far deeper commitment. It was not in any way an isolationist kind of prayer. It was a prayer that equipped him, in ways he always understood, to make him a pastor of souls. That is perhaps the most essential thing that I would want to say about him."

Cardinal Bernardin leads a life of prayer and wants everyone to know the enrichment of life that comes through prayer. This is what he had to say in reflections that he shared with his Cincinnati priests in 1981: "Prayer is a marvelous reality which can truly transform our lives. Its ultimate goal, of course, is to bring us into closer union with Jesus. In doing this, however, it also helps us to come to a better knowledge of ourselves and relate in a more loving, intimate way to others."

In the same message to his clergy he called Jesus a man of prayer: "The gospels tell us he prayed before all the important events in his life. Before beginning his public ministry, he went into the desert to fast and pray for forty days. And what intense prayer he experienced in the Garden of Gethsemane the night before making the supreme gift of himself to his Father on our behalf! St. Paul, in his letters, constantly focused on his need for prayer and the need of others."

To be a follower of Jesus Christ, the Archbishop of Cincinnati said to his priests, it is essential to be a person of prayer. "But," he continued, "it is important to know what prayer really involves. What kind of prayer were Jesus and the apostles talking about? What effect should prayer have on people, especially on us who are priests? Authentic prayer will have a tremendous effect in our lives. Contrary to what some have intimated, in no way should prayer insulate us from the real world. In no way should it become a crutch to avoid facing up realistically to life."

As Cardinal Bernardin shows in his own life of presiding at liturgical events, working at his office, catching up on necessary reading at home, driving his car to keep an appointment, eating his light lunch, drafting a memo, talking with a reporter, facing a television camera, shaving, celebrating Mass, putting his shoes on, answering the telephone or occasionally glancing at the TV set, prayer provides constant support and nourishment and is always at hand.

"Spiritual writers tell us there are many kinds of prayer," he wrote in 1981. "The four classical forms are vocal (that is, prayer expressed in words, either a fixed formula or one's own words), meditative, affective and contemplative. In the final analysis, however, each must pray in the way that best lifts his or her mind and heart to the Lord. Regardless of the particular method we use or the facility we may have developed, prayer, if it is genuine, must move us to a greater knowledge of ourselves. St. Teresa of Avila holds that one cannot grow closer to God without constantly growing in self-knowledge. Precisely for this reason, real growth in prayer involves a movement toward greater simplicity, that is, fewer words and thoughts." Cardinal Bernardin found this out through his own experience in prayer, just as a builder learns through experience how to construct a solid and lasting foundation.

That's implied by his friend Archbishop Kelly, who has observed him at close hand for many years, and in his own words and acts. It can be an overwhelming and even a jarring experience, as Cardinal Bernardin suggests in his reflections in Cincinnati: "As we move closer to God, everything within us which is not of God will be disclosed. If, on the other hand, we fail to recognize motivations or movements within us which are not of God, if we do not recognize the evil in us, that failure itself becomes an obstacle to closer union with the Lord. Often, of course, we are not fully conscious of what motivates us. It is very easy to fool ourselves."

The reflections have a permanent value and were published as a booklet by St. Anthony Messenger Press under the title "Called to Serve, Called to Lead." After he moved to Chicago, Cardinal Bernardin gave a copy to each of the some 2,400 priests in his archdiocese. It was devoured by men who had been waiting for just such guidance and challenge. Regardless of whether it was true, partially true, entirely true or not true at all, there was a feeling among Catholics and non-Catholics that there had developed within the Church of Chicago an anxiety about collective motivations and movements. There were divisions, groupings and regroupings, alliances and the dissolution of alliances. One person's enthusiasm became another person's suspicion. Motives were already being examined, but not always in the terms proposed in the Bernardin reflections: "Discovering our true selves can be a very painful experience. At first we tend to rebel when we confront our ugly side. This pain, however, is to be expected. We have been warned to expect the cross in our lives, and sometimes the cross comes not from outside us but from within."

Prayer has another vital dimension: "As it brings us closer to God, it also helps us to discover others. It involves a movement toward greater intimacy with others: with God first, of course, but also and in a particular way with other men and women."

Before he put those words onto paper Cardinal Bernardin experienced all that he described. In the words of Archbishop Kelly, "he became a true pastor; and by that I do not suggest that he wasn't one before, but that he deepened in an extraordinary way his roots. And he did this through prayer."

I asked Archbishop Kelly whether it was true that Archbishop Bernardin was called upon to be a pastor in Cincinnati in quite a different way from his pastoral calling in Washington, where his public life was so largely administrative. "Yes," answered Archbishop Kelly. "He described it to me one time. He talked about Confirmation. He had always confirmed graciously enough when he was a bishop in Georgia and in Washington, but he told me that when he went to Ohio and began to confirm the children who were his own children it had a completely different effect on him.

"The Sacrament of Confirmation has an impact not just on the recipient but on the one who administers it. I know that very well myself. As a bishop begins to have a deep awareness of a personal commitment to the people he is serving it comes across in Confirmation, and obviously in the Eucharist, at Ordination and at times such as that. And Bernardin began to have an experience of this in prayer, I believe; his prayer life was very much the support and the base for his sacramental administration."

It wasn't limited to that, though. Archbishop Kelly observed that his friend prayed over decisions he had to make, over public statements and positions, over his service to the Conference during his presidential years. "In all of that period prayer and his spiritual development began to take great leaps and bounds."

But the Bernardin experience with prayer was not confined to his chapel, his moments with the Rosary, his public or private prayers. Others were affected. I found myself taking a more prayerful approach to my work, turning to prayer as a help in reaching decisions, exposing my most unpleasant characteristics and most unworthy notions to the painful scrutiny of prayer, and all because of a man whose own life portrayed the reality of prayer the way a flame portrays the reality of heat. Knowing how he had shaken me up without saying a word to me on the subject, I knew that others must have felt something similar. I asked Archbishop Kelly what he thought about it. "It's true," he said.

"I pray that what happened to him will happen to me. God works differently with different people, so there's no one way that a person becomes a holy bishop. And I want to emphasize, I can't emphasize it enough, that his personal holiness is essentially related to his ministry. They are not two different things in his life. His ministry is sanctified and his prayer leads him to ministry. That's the way it is supposed to be with a bishop. St. Thomas Aquinas had that all spelled out in the 13th Century. It's as true today as it was then. It's marvelous to see that it happened in the life of one man I feel I know well enough to describe.''

But now, even as in the time of Aquinas, there are distractions that make it hard to live that kind of a life. There are thousands of persons seeking attention, asking for appointments, writing letters that must be answered. There are reporters and cameras, questions being asked and observations being made.

Even if you're a prince of the Church it isn't easy to keep the world in focus and to keep yourself in perspective when the world focuses so much attention on you, when privacy is so hard to come by. "Cardinal Bernardin seems to take that very well," Archbishop Kelly said. "I don't want to say that he's oblivious to public attention. He's very sensitive to the role media play in the life of the people these days and he wants to be present to his people. But he would never regard himself as a 'star performer.' He regards his ministry as central. Being in the media is a ministerial thing for him, not a personal thing.''

As one who was on hand for a number of Bernardin press conferences I knew that the Cardinal is somehow able to take the media for granted the way a person takes a brother for granted, with affection and understanding but without a need to be on stage or artificial. He doesn't try to present a special face to the media. His ability to see Christ present everywhere and to apply a Christian evaluation of others makes it unnecessary to be anyone other than himself.

That kind of knowledge and the extended arms that express it in spontaneous friendship do not lead to naive and uncritical judgments. Cardinal Bernardin is not a bewildered fellow who can be deceived at will, persuaded of anything through flattery or nudged into a false start by shallow enthusiasm. He seems to know what you're thinking. His intuition, honed no doubt by prayer, is a remarkably reliable guide. Nobody who knows him tries to put anything over on him. There are never any cards up his sleeve and he seems to know, with penetrating vision, when somebody else's shirt is stuffed.

He is sympathetic toward losers and whiners, forgiving toward the dishonest, but he doesn't enjoy their company. Maybe that helps to explain his success in management, which has both fiscal and spiritual dimensions.

As Archbishop Kelly put it, "He's just an enormously capable administrator and he doesn't seem to have to think about it. What he thinks about are his people, how to serve them best. The overwhelming managerial problems in Chicago, which might send me around the bend, are handled in a way that's just second nature to him. He's perfectly comfortable with all that. He is exactly where he ought to be. He is deepening his holiness, he is developing the episcopal ministry, experiencing it and, I think, loving it."

Chapter Six

CARDINAL Bernardin's view of his episcopacy, his idea of what it means to be a bishop whose service is expected to span the change of the centuries, tells quite a bit about who he is and how he thinks.

He knows as much about the American episcopacy as anyone around. He knows where the weaknesses are, but they are human weaknesses. He knows where the strengths are, and they are human strengths made stronger by Christ, whose Church they serve.

He also knows his brother bishops. After all, he's the only man in the country who was the operating chief, called general secretary, of both the National Conference of Catholic Bishops and the United States Catholic Conference and who later was elected president of those bodies. Nobody else has held both of those jobs, either one of which provides an overview of the Church in the United States, and a comprehension of its concerns, that is very special.

We know what Pope John Paul II thinks of Cardinal Bernardin as a bishop because the Pope spells it out in the formal appointment to Chicago. "Venerable brother," said the pontifical bull, "we have known you to be a bishop who understands how to build up a solid community of faith as God's gift drawing people ever closer to Christ the Lord. We have come to know you as a bishop who combines a deep priestly sense with prudence of action and a zeal to spread the Gospel with the greatest human sensitivity. It has been a great joy for us to observe your episcopate both in your work with the Episcopal Conference and in your ministry to the clergy and people of Cincinnati. We have become acquainted with your distinguished virtues.''

One man who knows the nature of the episcopacy with particular sensitivity also knows the Catholic Church in this country better than most Americans do. He is Archbishop Pio Laghi, Apostolic Delegate in the United States. My wife and I met Archbishop Laghi long ago in Jerusalem, where he was the Apostolic Delegate. That's not an easy post to fill. Tension is the lasting reality in the Middle East. Catholics are a small minority in Israel, a country with which the Vatican does not have diplomatic relations. Only a man of remarkable ability can handle the Apostolic Delegation in Jerusalem.

My next personal encounter with Archbishop Laghi was in Buenos Aires, after he had become the Papal Nuncio to Argentina. The Archbishop occupied an impressive official residence that had been presented to the Church by a wealthy Argentinian family, but he identified with Latin America's poor as readily as he worked with the powerful. He read airmail copies of *The Chicago Catholic* regularly in Buenos Aires before he was appointed to Washington, and so he was especially familiar with the problems of the Church in Chicago. During that period, he once said, he obtained most of his news about the Church in the United States from the Chicago weekly newspaper. In an article he wrote for that same newspaper at the time of Archbishop Bernardin's installation in Chicago's Holy Name Cathedral, Archbishop Laghi said: ''Archbishop Bernardin is not only a successor to his predecessors as archbishop, but like them, he is a successor to the apostles.'' He described Archbishop Bernardin as ''truly the 'vicar of Christ' for the Archdiocese of Chicago, leading, teaching and sanctifying in the name of Jesus, the Supreme Shepherd of the universal church and of the particular churches that make up the universal church."

He also wrote: "To the roles of leader and teacher we must add a third dimension of the episcopal office: the bishop as sanctifier of souls and spiritual center of the local church. The diocese is not a mere juridical entity or human organization—it is a living and growing portion of the Body of Christ, in and through which the faithful come into dynamic contact with the Lord. Since this is so, the bishop is not simply an administrator or an officer in an ecclesiastical chain of command. He is above all a visible, human principle of unity among his people in their lives of faith and worship."

The new Archbishop of Chicago recalled during his installation homily the description Jesus gave of a good shepherd, one who lays down his life for his people.

Said Archbishop Bernardin: "Some live this calling literally, shedding their blood as martyrs. Others live it in the unstinting giving of their time, their energy, their very selves to those they have been called to serve. Whatever the future holds for me, I pledge this day to live as a good shepherd who willingly lays down his life for you. I shall gladly spend my life in service of the spiritual mission to which the church calls me this day."

Reporters who try to keep up with his swift travels around Chicagoland know that Cardinal Bernardin does not bottle up his energy. Some wish he'd bottle part of it for the use of others. Even Father James Roache, the Cardinal's administrative assistant, told friends in a note received on the first day of April that he'd had no earlier chance to acknowledge their congratulations on his appointment the previous August. He was beginning to wonder whether an administrative assistant might need an administrative assistant of his own.

It wasn't long after the Bernardin installation in Chicago that his face appeared on the cover of *Time*, a mark of international attention that recognized his role on the widest of all stages. He was gaining interest in Washington and Moscow and other world capitals, along with interest in millions of homes everywhere, because of his chairmanship of an ad hoc committee drafting a pastoral letter on the issues of war and peace. That kind of attention seems normal to those who know him, especially the bishops of the country.

As his friend Archbishop Kelly of Louisville put it: "From my perspective, and I think I know the hierarchy fairly well, he is in a sense THE natural leader. The bishops understand that he must be in Chicago, that he can't be running the Church in the United States. But, whenever he speaks on the floor of the Bishops' Conference, everyone listens to what he has to say. I don't mean to say that they all stampede into following his leadership; it's not that kind of thing. But he is seen as a wise man, a man of experience."

Does that mean there's an authentic respect for him among his brother bishops? "Yes, and it is very deep and very universal. There are other bishops who also command wide respect, but Cardinal Bernardin's leadership has been extraordinary."

There are a good many people who think that the people of Louisville are fortunate in the kind of leadership they receive from their archbishop. Somebody recently told Archbishop Kelly that it was good to have somebody there who understood national issues. His answer: "I do have a deep awareness of what's going on in the Church in the United States and I try to be sensitive to the issues, but that's probably because I learned it from Bernardin. He is the one who manages to pull it all together, and although I don't want to use the word, he's the synthesizer."

That's not a quality to be taken for granted. Americans are not the only residents of the planet who tend to view all big organizations and institutions, including governments and the Church, with caution.

They tend to be even more cautious of institutions that are not essentially democratic, whether they are transnational corporations or hierarchical churches. Bishops in the modern world get further through leadership and example than by commands, and what they get is the opportunity to serve more people with a timeless message of expectation and hope. The Church has to justify itself in ways that didn't have to be thought about in the past.

The public at large, especially the non-Catholic majority, frequently perceives the entire Church by its institutional presence and the personalities of the Pope and the bishops. The Church has adapted to different centuries and societies and it isn't always easy on the bishops. Unless they live under civil or religious oppression, bishops may appear to have a big stake in keeping things as they are. Yet it was a gathering of bishops, summoned by one Pope and called again by his successor, who prayed and argued and struggled to produce the shakeup of the Church that's known as the Second Vatican Council. Cardinal Bernardin exemplifies what the Council had in mind when it talked about bishops and the Church.

Not even the Council could anticipate the reshaping of

American society by the media, especially television, and the resulting need for greater spontaneity and naturalness within the hierarchy. Today's bishop, facing a camera and a determined reporter, has no time to consult his advisers or to pull books off his library shelves before framing an answer. It may not be fair, it may not be right, it may not be proper, but it is a fact that Americans generally expect their bishops to be as familiar and as accessible as their governors and senators.

The bishops have inherited a Church which represents Jesus Christ to the entire world but which functions within a framework that dates in some respects to the Middle Ages. Bishops who are holy are equipped to summon the human community to holiness even if they know little about the techniques of television and press.

Cardinal Bernardin, his peers suggest, combines the precise qualities needed by a bishop who seeks to evangelize humankind, beginning at home.

Chapter Seven

FATHER Avery Dulles, S.J., wrote a book about *The Resilient Church*, observing that there's a need for resilience and adaptability and that there also are limitations. In 1983 Father Dulles continued to call for moderate reform of what's generally called the institutional Church and for that reform to be accomplished within the institution.

Father Dulles has explained, in another book, that just as the Church presents a variety of public images, the public grasp of those images varies according to what part of the public does the grasping. Conservative Catholics hear a radio news reference to the celebration of a Latin Mass in the Holy Land and see that as imaging a possible return to Latin in all liturgies everywhere. Traditional Catholics learn of Cardinal Bernardin's devotion to the Rosary and recall days when recitation of the Rosary was a part of almost every Catholic gathering.

Liberal Catholics wonder why a girl is not permitted to serve at the altar and why the ordination of women is not at hand. Middle-of-the-aisle Catholics read approvingly that the U.S. bishops suggest voluntary fast and abstinence on Fridays to underscore a commitment to peace and wonder whether other familiar and reassuring practices are on their way back.

Father Dulles has proposed that all Catholics think of the Church as a "community of disciples," a worthy thought that also is capable of raising expectations that conflict with one another. After all, the earliest disciples are frequently cited as authorities for keeping things as they were, for delving with either conservative or liberal fervor into the practices and teachings of the first Christians. When he wrote *The Resilient Church* Father Dulles saw the problem as finding a way to "achieve authentic modernization without a new Modernism and without destructive polarization."

Although he no doubt had other considerations in mind, the thoughtful Jesuit could have been describing the kind of efforts and achievements that characterize Cardinal Bernardin. His work in Cincinnati and Chicago has included attention to the updating of the way the institution operates.

He has been especially effective in overcoming polarization, which was a well established reality in Chicago when he arrived. He met with groups of Chicagoland Catholics, including liberals and conservatives, who had been largely ignored by his predecessor. He accepted an award from the Association of Chicago Priests, which was locked in battle with Cardinal Cody. He made the Presbyteral Senate effective by turning to it in trust and calling upon it for active cooperation. He talked with many, but he listened also. Cardinal Bernardin is a great listener. He understands that it takes two to tangle and it takes two to converse.

How did he get that way? There's always a temptation to practice a bit of psychology without a license, to do some amateur tracing of a person's early experiences with the idea of connecting them up with what happens later. Cardinal Bernardin has spoken of his boyhood in Columbia, S.C., where, in his words, he was the only Catholic kid on the block.

There are still a number of evangelicals, and not only in the South, who declare that Roman Catholics are not really Christians at all. All over the country, North and South and West, there are men and women of deep faith in Christ or of no faith in anything outside of themselves who see the Catholic Church as something foreign and evil. That's why the Catholic League for Religious and Civil Rights came into existence and has been so active in addressing the public, the media and the courts. It is possible to grow up in a Catholic neighborhood in Chicago without experiencing the social and economic discrimination that is known in other communities.

Francis P. Murphy, for many years managing editor of *The Worcester Telegram*, once leaned back in his chair in a quiet newsroom after the last edition had been locked up sometime after midnight and told me that even as he approached retirement age he remembered long-ago help wanted ads that specified "no Irish need apply." Before his death he saw Massachusetts change as the Catholic Church became more deeply rooted in the community, but he spoke of pockets of otherwise decent men and women who still shunned anything or anyone Catholic.

Frank Murphy was a saintly man who responded to affronts with prayer and forgiveness and tried to couple his forgiveness with forgetting, because he knew that one is not possible without the other. Even so, this man who became godfather to my son David, found it easier to forgive than to erase memories.

A person of holy instincts who grows up on the defensive in any way because of religious convictions is likely to develop the quality that Father Dulles describes as resilience. Such a person is eager to talk about issues that divide or separate, looking for an end to polarization. I've never discussed this with Cardinal Bernardin, who may not agree with my feeling that his early years may have influenced his inclination to pray about problems, to listen to what others are saying and to search for reconciliation on Christian terms. Cardinal Bernardin has never despised anyone because of the person's identity or how the person is described. He isn't programmed to hate a person because of race or religion. He just can't do it. This helps him, no doubt, in looking for solutions rather than for problems.

That may seem obvious, but there are men and women out there who find satisfaction in problems and who get a lift out of hating. Churches are still desecrated, synagogues are still plagued by the haters. Food in markets and medicine on the shelves of shops are still deliberately tampered with, bombs are found on aircraft, the poor are still robbed by hate-filled moral derelicts who stab and shoot victims who offer no resistance. Confrontation, violence, hatred exist on the most personal levels even as they do on a different level in international relations.

The Church addresses such problems on an individual, personal basis, calling upon each person to repent and to see Jesus as the model. It also addresses those problems on a local, national and world level. It works to overcome polarization and hatred, and Cardinal Bernardin is one of its most accomplished workers.

Some respond to early experiences by trying to get even, by violating the confidence and rights of others. But men and women such as Cardinal Bernardin, Frank Murphy, Mother Teresa and Dorothy Day respond with their own kind of affirmative action. Whatever the reasons, Cardinal Bernardin became recognized as a negotiator and mediator of unusual competence. His brother bishops have seen

this, routinely electing him to be a part of the World Synod
of Bishops where he has been routinely elected to the
Council.

Few people realize, said his friend Archbishop Kelly of
Louisville, that Cardinal Bernardin's voice is highly significant within the Council of the World Synod of Bishops.
"For years," Archbishop Kelly told me recently, "he has
been the one who helps pull the whole thing together at the
end. That's an enormously difficult task, given the
language and cultural differences of the participants. In
the sessions of the Synod Council which take place before
and after the Synod meetings themselves, his is a very
significant voice. He would be recognized as one of the few
top leaders in the whole effort. His role is never publicized
and that is good, because basically it is intended that the
group function, not the leadership."

As a member of the World Synod of Bishops, Cardinal
Bernardin was identified in another way with Pope John
Paul II, whose United States visit from Poland in 1976
came when Archbishop Bernardin was president of the
national conference of bishops. Karol Cardinal Wojtyla
figured prominently in Poland when Archbishop Bernardin spent ten days in a wide-ranging tour of that country.
Despite their different nationalities, the two men have
much in common in their personal spirituality, reliance on
prayer and application of unifying skills. There's a shared
experience also in their relationships with their people at
home, a sort of grace-filled development that enabled them
to serve comfortably on broader levels.

In Cincinnati Archbishop Bernardin interpreted all of
his life in terms of his service to his people and service
became the dominant factor in his life. In Cracow

something quite similar happened in the experience of Cardinal Wojtyla. Both were blessed with men of wisdom who gave them particular encouragement. They included John Cardinal Dearden, the former Archbishop of Detroit who was president of the National Conference of Catholic Bishops while Bishop Bernardin was its general secretary, and Stefan Cardinal Wyszynski, the Archbishop of Warsaw and Gniezno and the Primate of Poland.

Comparisons between Pope John Paul II and Cardinal Bernardin, striking as they are, should not be carried too far. Both are men of prayer, totally devoted to Jesus Christ, both are men of considerable native intelligence, with unusual skills in teaching and conciliating, both are natural leaders who want to see the Church through difficult times, adapting, creating and preserving.

But although they share some recreational interests, Cardinal Wojtyla was drawn to rugged mountains and challenging ski trails while Archbishop Bernardin was drawn to long walks and music. Both enjoy good food in limited amounts. Cardinal Bernardin may have little time to spend in the kitchen at 1555 North State Parkway, his official residence, but in the past he's been elected cook by popular acclamation. That was true in Washington and also in a borrowed home on Little Traverse Bay, an inlet of Lake Michigan in the northern part of the state of Michigan, where he's spent happy vacation days with Cardinal Dearden and other bishops. He keeps himself trim by eating lightly, but he still subscribes to *Gourmet* magazine. "My reputation as a chef is more of a myth than anything else," he told me during a Cincinnati interview, but he acknowledged that his fellow vacationers always asked him to take over the kitchen.

While others played golf he took walks. He went sailing
on the bay with others but did not think of himself as much
of a sailor. "I don't swim up there because the water's too
cold. I'm from South Carolina and I'm accustomed to
much warmer water." Whether he's on vacation or at
home he likes to read. He enjoys fiction but has to spend
so much time reading professional books that he doesn't
have as much time as he'd like for light reading. He's
almost a compulsive reader. That may provide some additional insight into his competence as a leader, arbitrator
and problem-solver. He is wide open to the thinking of
others, to ideas and suggestions.

He subscribes to the Jesuit weekly *America, The Tablet*
of London, the quarterly *Communio*, the Irish Dominican
magazine *Doctrine and Life, Worship, The Jurist, Commonweal, Time, U.S. News & World Report, National
Geographic*, the weekly documentary service *Origins* and a
number of others. He reads the daily NC News Service
packet and newspapers that include the Chicago dailies
and *The New York Times*. He's publisher of *The Chicago
Catholic*, which he and countless other bishops all over the
country read regularly. When he went for the first time as
Archbishop of Chicago to Washington to attend a meeting
of the National Conference of Catholic Bishops he was accompanied at some television interviews by Robert Beusse,
who was secretary of communication for the Conference
when Cardinal Bernardin was its general secretary. Bob
Beusse, now a consultant in New York City, recalled that
several bishops hailed the new Chicago Ordinary saying
about the same thing: "Congratulations, Joe. I read your
paper every week!"

Reading is as essential a factor as listening in developing a person who is conscious that a controversial issue may have more than one reasonable side. Through conversations, books, periodicals and meetings Cardinal Bernardin stokes the furnace of his intellect.

What he learns is related to his spirituality as swiftly and at times as unconsciously as a computer assembles information according to the way it has been programmed. Cardinal Bernardin is programmed to be reasonable, to submit ideas to a process of spiritual sifting, to overcome tendencies toward polarization.

Chapter Eight

CARDINAL Bernardin's ability to climb to his own spiritual heights in order to view all sides of difficult questions does not mean that he gives equal value to all positions or that he has no firm positions of his own. His positions are not only firm but they have been stated clearly. Nobody has to wonder what he thinks about controversial matters, whether they touch on race relations, the priestly ordination of women or the correctness of papal authority.

He communicates broadly and well and there is no reason for him to be misunderstood. He never says anything that leaves an ordinary person wondering what he meant by that. I mentioned that to Archbishop Kelly.

"Yes. You're right," he said. "He's always been a master of the written and spoken word, but particularly the written word. He has a tight discipline of his use of language. I envy that because it is not an easy quality to acquire. His careful use of language is always his own, even if he has consulted others in preparing his material. He's careful to clarify and refine and to see beyond possible misunderstandings."

He applies the same care to reading what others have written and to listening to what others are saying. He's unlikely to be in the situation that, according to one observer, was familiar to Franklin Delano Roosevelt when he occupied the White House.

President Roosevelt was said to listen to everybody, and to nod his head to show that he understood what he was being told. His visitors often thought that Mr. Roosevelt was nodding his head in agreement rather than to indicate understanding. This obviously could cause some painful misunderstandings.

He's careful in his conversations precisely in the way that he's careful in his writings and public addresses. Even during a noisy, energetic news conference it is almost possible to hear the semicolons and periods fall into place when Cardinal Bernardin speaks. Anyone who has something to say to him ought to know in advance that the Cardinal listens as carefully as he speaks, and he hears the semicolons, too.

This quality of clearness is evident in the lengthy pastoral letter on the issues of war and peace, which was drafted by a committee of United States bishops chaired by Cardinal Bernardin.

When my administrative secretary, Dolores Madlener, received a copy of Cardinal Bernardin's newspaper column written in longhand she sat down to type it at her customary freeway speed. She handed me both the Cardinal's draft and her copy of it and exclaimed in wonder that the handwriting included no scratching out or scratching over, no errors to be corrected, no lack of precision in any respect. If there had been any revisions, they were made before the author prepared his final longhand copy, developing his ideas step by step and concluding effectively.

Cardinal Bernardin actually thinks in an orderly and organized way, as his writing and speaking so plainly indicate. He's a totally reasonable man. Just what it feels like to be a fully reasonable man in a remarkably unreasonable world can probably be treated only in an autobiography, which the Cardinal may or may not be impelled to write eventually. This book is by no means a biography, although it builds upon biographical references. It is easier to understand what anyone says when there's some understanding of how the sayer thinks.

If there's such a thing as a born musician or painter there no doubt is a born educator and leader. Cardinal Bernardin is a born educator and a natural leader. He became chairman of the board of the National Catholic Educational Association in 1978, the year that Pope Paul VI named him a consultor for the Sacred Congregation for Catholic Education.

Even when he was overwhelmed by demands on his time and attention the week that the third and major draft of the war and peace pastoral was released to the public, even after battling a cold while making the strenuous rounds of Holy Week 1983, Cardinal Bernardin flew to Washington to address the National Catholic Educational Association's annual meeting.

He knows that education is an essential ingredient of personal development and of evangelization. He expressed that idea in an editorial for a special issue of the National Catholic Educational Association's publication, *Momentum*, in 1979 when he said: "The Church's total mission expresses itself in diverse ways yet is at the same time fundamentally simple. That mission is to evangelize—to bring the message of the Gospel to all people. And the mission is accomplished both by our teaching and our way of life.

"Our responsibility, therefore," he continued, "is to teach the Gospel not only to students in our Catholic schools but also to Catholic students in public schools, to Catholics who have not yet entered school, to Catholics who long ago finished school, to those who may never enter school, and, beyond that, to those who do not even claim membership in our Church. Our responsibility is to live our lives in such a way that we proclaim the Gospel of Jesus Christ by our very existence to all around us.''

And, he said, "It is evident at the same time that the history of the Catholic Church in the United States has been strongly shaped by the contributions of its schools. Thus, although the concern of the Church transcends the maintenance of a school system, we must not lose sight of the importance of that system to the total teaching mission of the Church.

"I am firmly convinced that our schools have proved a most effective instrument in the fulfillment of that mission. I do not subscribe to the thesis that, because conditions are different now from what they were when the schools were established, they are no longer needed. The purpose of our schools even in the past was much broader than simply 'protecting' the faith of children in a sometimes religiously hostile environment—as important as that was. Catholic schools have been a source of vigorous Catholic life in the United States.''

After he moved to Chicago, Cardinal Bernardin did not pull back from considering the possibility of school consolidations. He realized that it is not always possible to keep a particular school open. Neighborhoods change, populations shift. Public school officials respond to changes, closing some schools, consolidating others and sometimes building new ones. The closing of a school upsets students and parents, displaces teachers, affects a community in many ways. This is as true of Catholic schools as it is of public schools. Soon after he became the Archbishop of Chicago, Cardinal Bernardin began looking for an instrumentality to evaluate the situation and make plans for the future. He told me that this instrument must make it possible for the Church to get ideas and comments from those who will be affected.

The problems are often especially intense for Catholic schools because they do not receive, in the United States, the reasonable share of tax support that is taken for granted in some other democratic countries. This reflects the anti-Catholic bias of early public officials and judges, who distorted the concept of a separated church and state into a form of patriotic discrimination. Official attitudes toward the equal treatment of Catholic school children were in the 1980s just about where official attitudes toward black citizens were in earlier decades.

"Separate but equal" treatment was proclaimed by a cynical Supreme Court to justify giving less to black school children than to white school children. A similar cynicism, sustained by very old establishment hostility toward the Catholic Church, prevails in the field of education. Cardinal Bernardin has addressed this doctrine of discrimination, as we shall see further on.

Meanwhile he encourages excellence in Catholic education and works to get the most educational value for the money available. Cardinal Cody often remarked that during his tenure as Archbishop of Chicago more than $40 million was contributed to the operation of Catholic inner city schools, where the enrollment is largely black and by no means overwhelmingly Catholic.

The assertion by the Second Vatican Council that Catholic schools must adjust to the circumstances of changing times and conditions is easily accepted by Cardinal Bernardin. He has written of the profound effect that a better understanding of the Church and its mission, along with developments in education itself, will have on

Catholic schools. They justify their continued existence, according to the Cardinal, when they conform to high professional standards, nourish a living faith in the young and help the young to witness to their faith.

He rejects the idea that Church schools tend to create a Catholic "ghetto" view of the world. In his education editorial he said he was convinced that "in many respects our Catholic schools are in an excellent position to do much of the experimentation and adaptation necessary to develop more effective instructional programs. To accomplish this, however, we must do everything we can to maintain a viable system of Catholic schools. This will require, in many instances, greater efforts on our part."

Drawing upon his awareness of how public opinion is formed and appealed to, he said that the Church needs to "gain greater confidence and respect on the part of the public by letting people know about the many significant contributions the Church is making in so many areas, especially education. If those of us who are identified with the Church are convinced that it has something to offer in the field of education, we should give greater evidence of this to those around us. If the current renewal is to be realized, we surely need a certain amount of honest self-criticism. That criticism, however, should be positive and supported by a lively faith in the abiding presence of the Holy Spirit within the entire ecclesial community."

He continued: "For how can we convince others that they should have confidence if we appear to lack that confidence ourselves? Indeed, if we do not have confidence in the Catholic school as a time-tested, powerfully effective form of carrying on the Church's teaching mission, we cannot reasonably expect anyone to give of his or her talents and resources to advance this work. If this should happen, the entire teaching mission of the Church would suffer, not just the schools!''

That's laying it on the line. The teaching mission of the Church, so essential to its Christian presence, will suffer if confidence is undermined. In saying that, he knew that the schools have bumpy roads ahead. He said: ''It is understandable that this should cause a certain concern about the future among Catholic educators and the parents who send their children to our schools. But this only underlines the urgency of adopting a positive attitude toward the future and what it might bring. We must approach problems as challenges rather than threats.''

Cardinal Bernardin, who speaks from experience rather than textbooks on this as on many other subjects, insists that the education of a child begins at home. The efforts of parents set the tone for learning and accomplishment. In much of the modern world the media have a strong influence on the very young, even as they have on adults. The devastating acceptance of abortion as a practice with no greater moral significance than the extraction of a tooth is largely the result of media influences on adults.

But Cardinal Bernardin begins with the thought that a child's education begins at home, including rooms with television sets and radios in them, ''so that entry into school is more like passing from one room to another than from one world to another.''

He told members of the Catholic Principals' Association in 1983 that the teachers ''look and act like parents, though many of them are religious. The quiet of the classroom is like the busy quiet of a well-run home. The activities, in many cases, are indistinguishable from the activities of children in the home. In a sense, the children

in a parish school are at home and feel at home. This turn
has indeed been successfully negotiated. Thus it gives me
great pleasure to acknowledge the health and vitality of
our Catholic schools today."

Cardinal Bernardin also said: "It is generally
acknowledged that Catholic schools are viable and thriving
alternatives to the public schools and to other private
schools. More than mere alternatives, they are often seen
as models and trail-blazers in America's quest for excellence in education. Our schools continue to be strong in
the traditional areas of the three R's. Our students continue to be well disciplined. And our schools are open to
the innovative. Religion is stressed with great seriousness."

And he said: "What makes these accomplishments
especially noteworthy is that they take place in institutions
that honestly strive to be true communities of persons. In
an age of computerization, our schools foster a personal
approach."

He might have commented that the accomplishments are
noteworthy because they take place in institutions
—period. He didn't stop there, but many who express anxiety about all institutions have little idea how many they
depend upon. In addition to an institutional Church
there's institutional government, institutional education,
institutional health care and even institutional entertain-
ment on a network scale. Institutions are not by definition
undesirable.

It is the individual who interests Cardinal Bernardin,
however, within the institution of education: "It is one of
the glories of our schools that we unceasingly strive to treat
each child, parent, teacher and administrator as a person,
created in God's image and redeemed by his Son. 'In-

dividual help' and 'regard for each other' are not empty phrases. It is true that no school can take the place of a family. But in the spirit of the family, our schools see themselves as existing for the sole purpose of the making of persons, persons with the dual destiny of transforming the world and of living with God and his family forever.''

Cardinal Bernardin's family has always been important to him. His father died when Joseph was only six years old. The Cardinal told members of the Chicago, North Shore and West Suburban Area Serra Clubs during a dinner honoring seminarians in May of 1983 that his mother became both a mother and a father to him, that he looked to two first cousins who were medical doctors with such admiration that he decided to become a doctor.

After his graduation from a public high school in Columbia, where there was no Catholic high school for boys, he became a pre-med student on a scholarship at the University of South Carolina. It was after a year of study there, where his grades were good and he was happy with his surroundings, that his conversations with priests and his prayers and self-examination led him to begin the long road to the priesthood.

One argument in favor of strong Catholic schools in the United States is that they provide a choice, if not literally a free choice. Curiously, the United States has pioneered the practice of encouraging a state monopoly on education by making it costly to obtain anything other than a public education. The state monopoly on education was eagerly adopted by the Soviet Union, where conformity is the law. The development of young minds, the decisions about what is to be taught and, especially important, what is to be excluded, is predominantly in the hands of the government itself and agencies of government in the United States.

There's a slow but inevitable tendency toward conformity, uniformity and a need for official sanction of educational practices. Although this is carried out with patriotic fervor in education, the attitude would be instantly recognized for what it is if it were applied to other agencies of information, such as libraries, newspapers, television stations and lecture halls.

Cardinal Bernardin mentioned "consumerism" to the Catholic principals as something that has changed the relationship of parents to schools: "With a freedom unavailable to them in previous times, parents pick and choose the school their children will attend, and that freedom can be perceived as a threat rather than as one of many factors, all of which together constitute the very grounds of a fruitful relationship."

His interest in the handicapped led Cardinal Bernardin to speak to the principals about it. He mentioned a statement on the handicapped made four years earlier by the bishops: "Understandably, the main focus of the document was on the need to welcome the handicapped and their families into the mainstream of community worship in our parishes."

The bishops encouraged parishes to make their buildings readily accessible to the handicapped and touched on such practical matters before turning their attention to education. Cardinal Bernardin quoted what the bishops had to say about that: "Dioceses might make their most valuable contribution in the area of education. They should encourage and support training for all clergy, religious, seminarians and lay ministers, focusing special attention

on those actually serving handicapped individuals, whether
in parishes or some other setting. Religious education personnel could profit from guidance in adapting their cur-
ricula to the needs of handicapped learners, and Catholic
elementary and secondary school teachers could be provided in-service training in how best to integrate handicapped students into programs of regular education. The
diocesan office might also offer institutes for diocesan ad-
ministrators who direct programs with an impact on handicapped persons.''

The statement by the bishops continued: ''The coor-
dination of educational services within the dioceses should
supplement the provision of direct educational aids. It
is important to establish liaisons between facilities for
handicapped people operating under Catholic auspices
(special, residential and day schools; psychological services
and the like) and usual Catholic school programs. Only in
this way can the structural basis be laid for the integration,
where feasible, of handicapped students into programs
for the non-handicapped. Moreover, in order to ensure
handicapped individuals the widest possible range of
educational opportunities, Catholic facilities should be encouraged to develop working relationships both among
themselves and with private and public agencies serving the
same population.''

Cardinal Bernardin clearly meant to embrace that statement and to make it his own, while recognizing that it was
not simple to carry it out. His personal interest in reaching
out to the handicapped is shared, incidentally, by his administrative assistant, Father Roache, who has served as a
priest to the severely handicapped at Chicago Rehabilita-
tion Institute for years.

Any kind of education costs more than time and effort. It costs money. Cardinal Bernardin put it this way: "Education is the most expensive part of archdiocesan activities. How can we make our publics aware of how necessary their continuing support is? I said 'continuing support,' but I really should have said 'increasing support.' All of us are aware of how costs have escalated as we made the transition from schools exclusively staffed by religious to schools involving the full cooperation of large numbers of lay people, and we are aware that this transition has occured in a period of inflation accentuated by skyrocketing energy costs."

He acknowledged that many educators are concerned with problems of inequality: "Better schools in better neighborhoods frequently have better educational programs and charge less tuition than schools in poorer neighborhoods. How can we make it easier for parents with lower incomes to place their children in our schools?"

As long ago as 1978 he told members of a conference of religious educators in Springfield, Ill., that catechetics or religious education is an indispensable part of evangelization. He said: "Unfortunately, while there has been wide agreement on its purpose and importance, religious education has been the source of much tension within the Church in recent years." He said that catechetics is not reserved to specialists, insisting that "every Catholic should be a catechist according to his or her circumstances and opportunities."

The teaching of religion, which is one part of the work of Catholic schools, was so important to Archbishop Bernardin in Cincinnati that he prepared a memorandum for those who taught religion.

He included some words of caution: "Remember that you must teach the Church's teaching as the Church's teaching. Your primary task is not to teach your personal opinions or theological hypotheses, and in no case are you to present these as the Church's teaching. You must take care to present this teaching in a way that is appropriate to the age and maturity of those you teach, in a way designed to win acceptance from them of what you teach. Obviously you must be concerned for the growth in faith of your students, a goal that exceeds mere sharing of information. Sometimes to your own great disappointment you will find no evidence of this growth; you may even find signs of an atrophy or loss of faith. But even in the face of such frustration you must make every effort to provide your students with a clear and articulated presentation of what it is that the Church teaches. If the student chooses to reject that teaching, that is the student's responsibility. But he or she must be given an honest opportunity to learn what it is that he is rejecting."

Even some adults, it might be observed, miss out on that negative opportunity. Almost everyone has a friend or a relative who has rejected the whole Church of Christ because of a misunderstanding of what the Church teaches. Some have rejected the Church for trivial reasons, magnifying an offense experienced at the hands of a priest, sister or lay Catholic into a repudiation of Christ's Church. Others have isolated one element of Church experience or teaching, such as an unhappy moment in a parochial classroom or an unsatisfactory encounter with a preoccupied pastor, building it into a renunciation of what at least passed for faith and commitment.

Graham Greene touched on that need for accurate information about the Church in an interview with Marie-

Francoise Allain that appears in *The Other Man.* Although he is a better novelist than theologian, Graham Greene attributed his conversion to Catholic Christianity to his intellectual searching for information about God. Once he had mastered that understanding he was ready to accept the reality of miracles and to embrace what others called superstition.

While in Cincinnati, Archbishop Bernardin told religious educators that he was interested in three specific problems. He identified them as permanence and change in Church teaching, the authentic doctrine of Catholic faith and dissent from the moral teaching of the Church.

He said: "We have all heard remarks in recent years that if some long deceased grandparents came back to life, they would not find the same Church in which they worshipped. The use of English at Mass, the altar facing the people, the joyful congregational singing and musical instrumentation with guitars and flutes, the involvement of lay persons in reading and in distributing Holy Communion, and the simplicity of church decor would all confuse them mightily. Yet they would also have been confused to attend a Third Century Eucharist in the catacombs or a Tenth Century Mass in a monastic church. Clearly the Church does change in her 'life style'; yet none of the changes just listed indicate any substantial change in the 'deposit of faith' we are discussing."

Those external changes reflect a new emphasis and awareness of certain beliefs, he acknowledged. They include the central nature of the Eucharistic sacrifice over other forms of prayer in the Church, the proper participation of the laity and the importance of "relevance and intelligibility" in worship. Yet, he said, "such new emphases and insights do not represent new doctrines but the fruit of serious efforts at renewal within the Church."

He talked about theologians. He said that they "provide a great and necessary service to the Church, keeping her intellectually alive and in touch with the realities of the world in which she exists. Yet theologians do not teach officially in the name of the Church, as theologians, but in their own name. Therefore their teaching as it interprets revealed truth is always subject to the reviewing judgment of the Church's bishops who are the official teachers in the Church."

He said later in the same document that "such basic doctrines as the divinity and humanity of Christ, the Real Presence of Christ in the Holy Eucharist, the sacramental forgiveness of sins in the Sacrament of Penance and the charism of infallibility by which the Church preserves pure and undefiled her deposit of faith can never be substantially changed." Cardinal Bernardin stated it plainly. Some things can never be changed. Other things, the externals, can and sometimes should be changed.

He commented that the renewal stimulated by the Second Vatican Council has caused all Catholics to experience "not only a dissatisfaction with the methodology of much of our previous religious education but also a desire to teach the faith in a more ecumenical context and in a language more understandable and less technically theological. Unfortunately, this has created for some the impression that the content of our faith has substantially changed or that it makes little difference how Christians express their faith as long as they are sincere. These are false impressions."

He cautioned that "we must never lose sight of our belief in the doctrinal integrity and unique role of our Catholic Church in God's plan of salvation." He explained that "the Church which assures us of the divine inspiration of the Bible itself is still the teacher of authentic doctrine today as in the days of forming biblical canon and of inspired writing."

Dissent from the moral teaching of the Church, he said, is not to be taken lightly: "Dissent means the refusal to assent or to accept. Since faith in Jesus calls for acceptance of him, his teaching and his Church, Christianity itself is based on assent." He said also that "to deny defined doctrines of the faith is to espouse heresy in some form or other."

He spoke of the Ten Commandments as part of the "deposit of faith" which the Church inherits and teaches infallibly. He said that it can "readily be argued that the Church has infallibly taught the indissolubility of Christian marriage."

This was followed by a distinction: "On the other hand, while the Church's opposition to contraception has been unanimous teaching throughout history it may be questioned whether this teaching has been understood as divinely revealed. For this reason the theologians today who dissent from the teaching about the universal moral evil of contraceptive intercourse in marriage suggest that such dissent does not violate divine faith although it disagrees with what is called the 'authentic, non-infallible magisterium.'"

And, he said: "It is important to note that theologians who dissent from *Humanae Vitae* are not usually considering contraception as morally good or indifferent. Rather they are arguing for specific cases of justifiable use of contraception where the physical evil of contraception is overshadowed by the good achieved in conjugal intercourse."

He went on to observe: "Some theologians are using the

same methodology to justify specific instances of premarital sexual intercourse, homosexual activity, masturbation and even direct abortion. Yet in all these areas the Church has consistently taught that these actions are always wrong in themselves, even though subjectively persons are not always fully responsible for that wrong."

He recognized that living up to the highest expectations of a Christian is not easy: "The moral and physical suffering that we experience in living by the objective norms of the Church becomes redemptive suffering when we suffer with Christ in our quest for moral integrity." He reminded religious educators of this: "Chastity can be taught as the virtue enriched by divine grace which aids human persons in expressing sexual activity within the order and purpose for which God intended it. Chastity may seem impossible or unrealistic in a secular ethic but we believe it belongs to the process of personal fulfillment and perfection that Christ taught for both the married and the unmarried state."

This is a formidable occupation in a society that encourages sexual exploitation and appears to reward those who ridicule moral integrity. Publishers, theaters and television stations profit richly from their success in mocking the Church and denying the certainty of moral standards. They make money on the young and target much of their material toward the young.

It takes a firmly convinced, spiritually assured teacher of religion to overcome the appeals of a life without rules. It is as tough a prospect for a teacher of Christian doctrine working with a group of youngsters in the living room after school as it is for an archbishop. Yet it is the archbishop who feels responsible for everybody, including the teacher and the kids.

Chapter Nine

CARDINAL Bernardin's instincts to educate began long before he started work on his master's degree in education at the Catholic University of America in Washington. In 1983 I told a group of theologians and journalists at Marquette University in Milwaukee that Cardinal Bernardin's sense of what it means to be an archbishop includes a compulsion to teach. He even teaches journalists, something that stirs as much wonder as admiration in the heart of anyone who's ever been a journalist or ever worked with one.

During that Milwaukee lecture, which was sponsored by the Marquette College of Journalism and Department of Theology, I commented that long before he became a Chicagoan, Cardinal Bernardin was known to theologians and journalists. They knew he would work with them to the outer limits of honesty and integrity. They saw him as a committed advocate of truth in all disciplines and professions, a representative of the best there is in church leadership.

Anybody who teaches well, whether by instinct or professional training or a fortunate combination of the two, stays more than a chapter ahead of the class. Cardinal Bernardin and other good teachers soak up information, then organize it with the happy zeal of crossword addicts before they speak or write. Dean James Scotton of Marquette's College of Journalism told me that teaching only looks easy. As he said it a couple of members of his faculty who are full-time journalists and part-time instructors nodded in agreement.

If the Cardinal makes it look easy, it is because he takes the trouble to know what he's talking about. This was plain even at the time of his ordination in 1952. John and Louise Miglarese mentioned it while they were in Rome for the 1983 Consistory. They are originally from Cincinnati but are long-time residents of South Carolina, where Cardinal Bernardin was born and acquired a softness of tone that he's never lost.

The Miglareses flew to Rome with their son, Father Sam Miglarese. They spoke happily of their early days with a young Father Bernardin, who was assigned to Charleston but drove 50 miles many weeks to offer Mass in Walterboro, then 25 miles further to a mission church in Hampton, where the Miglareses lived.

Henry Tecklenburg, Jr., who became chairman of the South Carolina State Ports Authority, lived diagonally across from the Charleston cathedral when the young Joseph Bernardin was ordained. He was on hand in Atlanta when Bishop Bernardin was installed as auxiliary, in Cincinnati when Archbishop Bernardin was installed, in Chicago when Bernardin succeeded Cardinal Cody, then in Rome for the red hat ceremony in the huge audience hall in Vatican City.

A couple of old friends peered at the platform to try to spot Cardinal Bernardin when he entered. "That's Joe," one cried out in excitement. "I can tell by his walk." His walk, his instinctive reaching out to grasp the hand of a listener while he speaks intently, his smile that seems to embrace strangers, his gentle speech and intense concern with people around him, are all familiar to his old South Carolina friends and relatives. In Rome they said that he hadn't changed. He'd always looked for his answers in

Scripture and prayer, he always drove 75 miles to meet someone's need. Even in altar boy days he was a good student.

He remained a good student at the University of South Carolina and after he changed to the seminary. "I can't look at him or think about him today without tears coming to my eyes," one woman declared matter-of-factly in her South Carolina accent while she spoke with friends in St. Peter's Square.

Iris Levy went to high school with Joe Bernardin. She grew up and married Dr. Sam Balcum of Columbia, the Cardinal's hometown. She missed a word during the Vatican ceremony. "What did that priest say?" she asked. "Go in peace," she was told. "Oh," said Mrs. Balcum, "that's just like our shalom." From his earliest days, Joseph Bernardin had no trouble with interfaith understanding.

Most of the Cardinal's visiting relatives and friends stayed in Rome's Leonardo da Vinci Hotel, which had been headquarters many years earlier for Cardinal Cody's Conclave visitors. Cardinal Bernardin and his clerical associates were at Villa Stritch, where the Chicago archbishop spent many late hours working on homilies and other formal expressions of his teaching mission.

Any Consistory is an overwhelming time for the new cardinals. Cardinal Bernardin lunched with Pope John Paul II, dined with Archbishop Paul Marcinkus, attended a luncheon as the guest of William Wilson, President Reagan's personal representative to the Holy See, celebrated Mass, met with reporters, picked up thoughts about the collective pastoral letter on war and peace that was to be voted upon by U.S. bishops the following May.

Cardinal Bernardin and about 60 of his relatives and friends were received in audience by the Pope, climbing Alpine stairs that led to the interior of a formidable palace protected by smartly-trained and colorfully-uniformed Swiss guards.

Even the lengthy stairways looked shorter to those who had waited outdoors in the brisk Rome evening. Temperatures at night dropped to as low as 32, noticeable even to Chicagoans after an exceptionally mild winter at home, raising goosebumps among the South Carolina and Georgia Bernardins and friends. In the audience hall a Pope in white greeted cardinals in scarlet, spoke with bishops and priests and laity in the Bernardin party, blessed all and moved on. Visitors left the palace thinking that marble floors are certainly palatial, but royally unyielding to tired feet.

One of the last to reach the pavement of St. Peter's Square at the base of the splendid Bernini columns was Cardinal Bernardin, awaited by reporters and film crews. Television lights burst through the gray chill of evening; the cardinal paused for another interview before hurrying on to dinner with Archbishop Marcinkus, administrator of Vatican City and head of the Vatican bank.

There was to be one more night in Rome before the long flight home. Each of the guests at a reception at the North American College received a personal greeting from the Cardinal, who has the extraordinary knack of giving his total attention to anyone with whom he's talking, no matter how much conversation or how many distractions surround him. This is not a small skill and it is not a common one. I'll have more to say about that later on.

What does it mean to be a priest in Rome? When I made

my first visit to the Holy Land in the Sixties I felt an almost physical impact, a scooping up into something that I could not comprehend; it was as though I had stepped onto ground that transmitted invisible waves of a real presence of Christ the way a radio station might transmit waves of sound. After I returned home I made a nuisance of myself whenever I ran across a Jewish friend. If I, a Christian, could be so overwhelmed by the Holy Land, how could I not try to persuade every Jew I knew to drop everything and head for Israel?

On a later trip with my wife I found that the mysterious pull of the Holy Land was just as compelling for her and not at all diminished for me. Rome is a stirring experience for Christians, too, and as a layman I've always thought that it must be especially magnetic for priests. Cardinal Cody visited Rome about a hundred times, obtaining spiritual nourishment on each visit. I'm fortunate to have been in Rome many times over a period of many years and the pull remains as powerful as ever. What must it mean to a priest, especially to one who is going to Rome to become a prince of the Church?

There was a time when it was almost as difficult for a priest to become a layman as for a layman to become a priest. Actually the laicization of a cleric dispenses a person from the ordinary duties of his office and usually from the vow of celibacy, but the laicized person does not lose his sacramental powers. There is something special about the priesthood that is not universally understood, especially by those who are not Roman Catholics. Cardinal Bernardin's recognition of the laity is vividly evident.

His understanding of priesthood and its unique place in human history is significant, especially during a time of declining vocations to the religious life in general. His personal example seems likely to influence young men to take a fresh look at ordained service to the community. Being a cardinal, he quipped, means that you sit in a chair with arms during Vatican meetings while lesser folk sit in chairs without arms. But being a priest means more than any form of respect can symbolize.

Shortly after I moved to Chicago I mentioned to Cardinal Cody one morning that I was anxious about taking my test for an Illinois driving license, because I'm the sort of person who gets anxious about taking any kind of test. Some of my teachers will acknowledge that I probably have good reason to be anxious about tests. Cardinal Cody told me to relax. He'd taken the driving license test, he told me. "All they did was send a man out to have me drive around my parking lot and ask a few questions," he said.

I tried to explain that "they" were not going to send a man out to give me my test in my parking lot. The courtesies that go with priesthood, and especially with the red hat, are generally earned the hard way.

Cardinal Bernardin has often talked about his awareness of priesthood, that special service to the Lord and to the community, as he did in 1978 when he spoke of Pope John Paul I. "In his short pontificate there was not enough time to make any important decisions or issue any momentous statements," the man who was then Archbishop of Cincinnati told religious educators in Springfield, Ill. "Yet, in the thirty-four days he was Pope, the entire world responded positively to his warmth and his down-to-earth approach to life. Simply by being the man he was—a simple, compassionate pastor—he reflected the Lord's goodness and love in a marvelous way."

How this thinking permeates his life was told in a revealing talk to some 150 Chicagoland priests involved in Hispanic ministry. It was given in February of 1983 at St. Mary of the Lake Seminary in Mundelein, drawing tears as well as a standing ovation.

Cardinal Bernardin told the priests that he had been ordained thirty-one years: "And it took me nearly twenty-five years to realize that my busyness wasn't really what the Lord and the people wanted (no matter how many demands the latter seemed to be making). It took me nearly twenty-five years to realize that, if I wanted to be a truly successful priest and bishop, I had to put Jesus first in my life—not merely in theory but also in practice.

"It was about six years ago—with the help of some priests, all younger and holier than I—that I learned how to pray; that I made the determination to find the time each day to devote to prayer. It was then that I let go of Joe Bernardin and grabbed on to the Lord. And since that time everything has changed!

"Don't misunderstand: the human condition which I share with you and everyone else has not disappeared. Externally, my responsibilities—the pressures—have increased. Internally, I confront the same difficulties as before. I must come to grips with my sexuality and what it means for me as one who has committed himself to celibacy for the sake of the Kingdom. I experience loneliness at times, despite a life crowded with people and events.

"I experience anxieties caused by a fear that I will not live up to others' expectations. My feelings are hurt when others misunderstand or criticize what I do. I am frustrated when my best efforts seem to accomplish little or nothing. I am plagued at times by a certain spiritual dryness or aridity, a sense of abandonment—even when I am desperately searching for the Lord in prayer. I suffer a loss of morale when people seem not to notice what I am doing; when they take me for granted. So the human condition has not changed. I experience all the same difficulties as before.''

This was a remarkable acknowledgment for a man who had not long before been given a thunderous welcome to his new Archdiocese, who had just received from the hands of the Holy Father the symbolic red hat of an extraordinary churchman.

It shared some of the admission of human problems that was expressed by one of his predecessors, George William Cardinal Mundelein, but it was not the Bernardin style or the style of the contemporary Church to repeat Cardinal Mundelein's kind of plea to the clergy.

In his 1983 book *Corporation Sole*, Edward R. Kantowicz quotes from the first Mundelein address to Chicago priests: "I am going to make mistakes. But I am your archbishop and I look to my priests to cover up my mistakes, not to expose, to discuss or to criticize them. To whom else can I look for such consideration? Your archbishop is the one man in this town who is constantly in the spotlight. Shield him as much as you can.''

Cardinal Mundelein served from 1916 to 1939, making some lasting contributions to the Church in Chicago and throughout the country. But circumstances change and so do styles of leadership, as Cardinal Bernardin demonstrated when in 1983 he spoke on the snow-covered grounds of the seminary built in a town named after his predecessor.

Something has changed, Cardinal Bernardin told his

priests, and what has changed is the fact that he learned how to deal better with the difficulties that he experiences: "Now it is no longer I, alone. It is the Lord and I, together. Indeed, it is my weakness and vulnerability that become my strength because then I no longer pretend that it is I who am calling the shots or am in control, but the Lord Jesus. And this, my brothers, brings me back to the purpose of the meeting which we are concluding today. We are here to reflect on our ministry to our Hispanic brothers and sisters."

In the final analysis, the Cardinal said, "my best contribution or gift is to help you grow in the Lord who alone can bring your efforts to fruition. My best gift to you is myself. Beneath the titles of archbishop or cardinal is a man—Joseph Bernardin—who is weak and sinful like you, in need of affirmation and support, at times full of doubts and anxieties, very sensitive, easily hurt and frustrated.

"But this Joseph Bernardin is also a man of great faith, one who is in love with the Lord, one who struggles each day—sometimes with little obvious success—to decrease so the Lord can increase in him, a man whose life is full of crooked lines but who is willing to let the Lord write straight with them. My brothers, know that this man, Joseph, has a great affection for you. Know that when you fail, he understands. Know that when you do crazy things that bring grief to others (as he himself does so frequently), he forgives you. Know that as you try to cope with the realities of life—both personally and ministerially—he is at your side, ready to help in every way he can.

"Know that when you succeed, he smiles and shares your joy and satisfaction. Know that when you are sad, hurt, demoralized, he cries with you. Know that this man,

Joseph, loves you; that he is proud of you; and that, for
the sake of the Lord, he is ready and willing to give his life
for you!''

The head of a mammoth archdiocese has a lot to smile
about and a lot to forgive. Cardinal Bernardin's reliance
on Jesus for strength and guidance is apparent to those
who work closely with him and the effects of that reliance
are known to all who worship in Chicagoland. It is known
in particular by the editor of Cardinal Bernardin's
newspaper, who so often fails in making Christ live in its
pages and govern its operation.

Ordination is a sacred rite that enables young men to
share in Christ's priestly ministry. It is one of the warmest
experiences for any bishop. The man to be ordained is ex-
horted in the ceremony "to serve Christ the teacher, priest
and shepherd in his ministry which is to make his own
body, the Church, grow into the people of God, a holy
temple.'' The Roman Pontifical then says that "by con-
secration he will be made a true priest of the New Testa-
ment, to preach the Gospel, sustain God's people and
celebrate the liturgy, above all, the Lord's sacrifice.''

In a 1981 homily for ordinations at Cincinnati's
Cathedral of St. Peter in Chains, Archbishop Bernardin
said that "the work we do as priests is not our own, but
that of Jesus. It is in his name, and his alone, that we
minister.'' He said that "the work we do in Christ's name
is basically a service for others.'' Then he told the candidates: "You must be really convinced that you have
made a lifelong commitment to the Lord and to the
Church. By this I mean a firm determination that, for the
rest of your life—no matter what the difficulties might be,
you will stand by your solemn promise to serve the Lord as
a priest.''

In words that took on a personal glow in his talk to the priests engaged in Chicago's Hispanic ministry a couple of years later, he said this: "It is easy enough to say that you have made such a commitment. The emotion of the moment is enough to carry you through.

"But what about a year from now, or ten years, or twenty? Will you have the will to persevere when you are faced with apathy or even rejection on the part of those whom you have tried to help? When boredom, failure and loneliness play havoc with your own personal spirituality and peace of mind? When the troublesome moments come, as indeed they must, will you be willing to place yourselves in the hands of the Lord and let him be your strength, even though there may be no visible sign that he is at your side to support and sustain you? Will you have the courage always to honor your commitment, confident that God will give you the grace to persevere?"

Why talk that way on such a happy day? "I am simply being realistic. I want you to understand that you are not so different that you will never experience the cross in remaining faithful to your commitment." He recalled the joys of his priestly and episcopal ministry and said that his faith and commitment were never stronger nor was his outlook ever brighter.

"I can tell you, however, that I have not been spared the frustrations, the loneliness and the spiritual dryness which at times make you wonder whether you can continue, whether the Lord is asking more than can be expected of a weak human being."

In another ordination homily he talked about what a total commitment means to a priest: "It demands a simpler life style and a greater outreach to others, especially the poor and the oppressed. It calls for taking positions on

justice, war and peace, the dignity of life and the right to
life which run counter to the pressures and expectations of
our contemporary society. It means emptying ourselves of
all those tendencies within us that draw us away from God.

"For us priests, total commitment to the Lord also
means living the life of celibacy with such integrity that it
becomes evident to others that we see and cherish it as a
reality which has far greater meaning and richness than a
mere law or discipline. It is truly an offering—a
sacrifice—freely and publicly given for the sake of the
kingdom of heaven, one which enhances the effectiveness
of our witness to the Gospel and the fruitfulness of our
ministry, one which is an encouragement to others to see
sexuality as a wonderful and noble gift from God rather
than simply an object for pleasure or manipulation."

He said in that 1981 homily that the requirements of
priesthood "will set us apart from others and even stir up
hostility against us. It will cause people to think we are
strange, out of step, naive."

There is little that's naive about Cardinal Bernardin, as
even governments have found out. The Reagan Administration may have thought so when it sought to hail the
publication of the third draft of the pastoral letter on
war and peace, drafted under Cardinal Bernardin's chairmanship, as a caving in to Administration objections to the
second draft. All of that will be the subject of another
chapter. It will be shown that although a few reporters who
had not read the second and third drafts all the way
through may have accepted the view of an Administration
that seemed to speak from Madison Avenue instead of
from Pennsylvania Avenue, government officials knew
that no moral judgments had changed.

For Cardinal Bernardin to have altered his moral judgments out of political considerations would have been to deny the life he was living as a priest. In the fall of 1982 he said in a Mass at St. Mary of the Lake Seminary: "Your goal as priests will be to proclaim God's word which is so central to our lives if we are truly to be his people; to make it come alive for the people whom you will serve; to help them incarnate this word in all its richness in their daily lives so that they will become, in fact, one body, giving witness to God's goodness and love for all the world...."

Cardinal Bernardin then addressed himself to the essential question of spiritual formation, the silent shaping of a young man's spiritual muscles: "Even though the priesthood is not dependent on personal worthiness, with the grace God gives to us and, within the framework of our human limitations, we must strive to be as worthy as possible. We must be committed to prayer which brings us into close union with the Lord. We must be honest and humble, never exalting ourselves but always placing the needs of our people first, always ready to serve them.

"The driving force in our lives must be love—not a sentimental, overly permissive kind of love, but a love that demands firmness and courage at times; a love that will not permit us to turn our backs on others even when they offend us or try our patience. As men who have willingly embraced the charism of celibacy, we must strive to be pure in mind and body for the sake of the kingdom. We must learn how to live with the pain that comes from being a sign of contradiction as we proclaim to our people a Gospel which is opposed to so many of the values of our contemporary society."

Elsewhere he has spoken of the "extraordinary gift of

priesthood," telling priests that "we are part of a much
larger reality than ourselves. We are part of the Church.
And the Church is essentially a mystery which cannot be
fully captured by human thought or language, which cannot be altered or adjusted to fit any purely human model."
He said in a homily to priests on April 10, 1979 that "it is
within the mystery of the Church, in which the human and
divine meet in the person of Jesus, that the priesthood of
the New Covenant is situated."

He went on to say that "any attempt to explain the
priesthood independently of the mystery of Christ and his
Church will be fruitless. Any attempt to tear the
priesthood away from its roots will end in disillusionment
and failure on our part. It is precisely the effort
—sometimes made innocently and unknowingly—to explain the priesthood in purely human terms, to rob it of its
essentially spiritual task of reconciling the human family
with the Father, that has caused confusion and pain among
the best of us."

He quoted from an address given by Pope John Paul II
to the priests of Rome: "Let us not deceive ourselves that
we are serving the Gospel if we try to 'water down' our
priestly charism through exaggerated interest in the vast
field of temporal problems, if we wish to 'secularize' our
way of living and acting, if we cancel even the external
signs of our priestly vocation."

Cardinal Bernardin said that priests must be men of
faith in constant communion with the Lord through
prayer. "Otherwise we will begin to dry up and our
ministry will suffer. The message we preach and the
sacraments we celebrate are intended to be encounters with
the Lord for ourselves and for our people, but what cold

encounters they will be if we ourselves do not really know the Lord, if we ourselves have not experienced his love and goodness in that communion with him we call prayer." Characteristically, he put heavy emphasis on the Bible and its place in the life of the Church.

Priests must, he insisted, be "well versed in Scripture and in our Catholic theological tradition." He said that priests "must know—and be able to explain to others—why we do certain things. It is only when we become disconnected from our theological heritage—a heritage, incidentally, which under the guidance of the magisterium constantly grows and develops—that our ministerial actions lose their full meaning and significance. It is only when we separate ourselves from our theological moorings that we become superficial in our words and actions. This is why prayerful reflections on the Scriptures and serious theological study are needed on a continuing basis for all of us."

From the beginning of his work as a bishop, Cardinal Bernardin has been conscious of the communion which exists between the bishop and his priests. He has said that this reflects "the deeper union between Christ, the eternal high priest, and all his human counterparts who continue his saving ministry."

He has spoken of the priesthood of all believers, something that is shared by all who are baptized, whether laity or clergy. He has reflected on Peter's letter in which he tells candidates for baptism: "You, however, are a chosen race, a royal priesthood, a holy nation, a people he claims for his own to proclaim the glorious works of the One who called you from darkness into his marvelous light."

He included those words in a letter on the ministerial priesthood written on the fifteenth anniversary of his episcopal ordination in 1981. In that letter he presented some thoughts about the specific identity of priests, and anyone who wants to understand Cardinal Bernardin must understand those thoughts: "Like Jesus, we are chosen, anointed and sent forth to proclaim the good news of salvation in the kingdom which he announced. Our calling and anointing, which enable us to share in a special way in the power of God's Spirit, give us our identity as priests.

"We are instruments who minister 'in the person of Christ.' We have a unique role in the Church because we are called to be 'an effective sign and witness to the Church's faith in the reconciling Christ, who works through the Church and through the one whom the Church has sent to be the steward of its gifts and services.' This special identity, however, does not make us better than others, nor does it entitle us to special privileges. But it does signify who we are, whom we represent, what our mission is and what demands are made of us in regard to spiritual growth and commitment to others.

"Moreover," the cardinal continued, "this priestly identity is not superficial or something we can hide or discard. It is not a part-time reality. No matter where we are, what we are doing, whom we are serving we are 'marked' men who must openly give witness to the special mission Christ has shared with us. To try to hide or downplay this special calling—this divine election—by espousing values or adopting a life style contrary to those evident in the life and ministry of Jesus, would be to cloud our true identity and ultimately to betray our vocation."

Cardinal Bernardin's view of priesthood is thoroughly

contemporary, generous if not liberal. Obviously he places heavy emphasis on the sacred character of priesthood while understanding, through his own experience, the temptations of an undemanding secularity. As will be seen, he has close ongoing relationships with the laity, Catholic and otherwise. Yet he affirms in his life and words the unique nature of the priesthood, which he understands to be a calling both inspired and lasting.

Almost as soon as he reached Chicago he met with his priests at Holy Name Cathedral. He gave this personal accounting in the course of a homily at evening prayer with the clergy: "My father Joseph, who came to America from the province of Trent in Northern Italy, was a stonecutter. Though he died when I was only six, I remember him.

"With the loss of my father, I became even closer to my dear mother, Maria, and my sister, Elaine. I was very blessed to grow up in a family full of love, faith and a willingness to work hard. I had long wanted to be a doctor, but in 1945 I decided to become a priest. I have very happy memories of the years I spent in Charleston after ordination and in Atlanta as pastor of Christ the King Cathedral parish. Two of the most influential priests in my life have been the late Archbishop Paul Hallinan, whom I served as chancellor in Charleston and later as auxiliary bishop of Atlanta, and Cardinal John Dearden, who was president of the bishops' conference when I was general secretary.

"I have benefited greatly from my experiences as president of the National Conference of Catholic Bishops, as a delegate to several synods and as a member of the Congregation for Bishops. But the greatest blessing in my priesthood were the ten years during which I was privileged to serve as Archbishop of Cincinnati."

Then he told the priests: "As to my personal tastes and habits, I am quite ordinary. I do like music. My favorite is classical, especially opera. I am credited with being a good cook but that is somewhat exaggerated. One of the main difficulties in recent years has been the lack of time needed to develop whatever culinary skills I might have. Also, I do not want to regain the weight I lost several years ago. My friends say I am a workaholic, but I do not think I am. If I do work hard, it is more because I like what I do than because of compulsion. Yet I do not consider myself indispensable. I do take time for recreation and refreshment. At the end of the day I enjoy a brisk walk and an easy conversation with a fellow priest."

He spoke warmly and with appreciation of Chicago priests, and said that he had known many before leaving Cincinnati. He said that the priesthood "is not a job. The priest is not a functionary, not a general practitioner, not a poor man's psychologist. True, many things about priestly ministry resemble a job. Priests ask, for example, 'Where are you working now?' We have work schedules, organizations, a distinctive uniform. But still the priesthood is not a job."

Here's what it is: "The priesthood is a passionate commitment, a fiery-eyed vision and an insatiable thirst for holiness and practical justice. The priest is called to be challenger, enabler, life-giver, poet of life, musicmaker, dreamer of dreams. He must be a man of deep personal faith, conformed to Christ, a man who loves the Scriptures, draws sustenance from the sacramental life of the Church, and truly knows the community with and for whom he offers sacrifice.

"A priest is a man with a clear sense of his own self, one

who strives to develop all his natural talents to the limit for the good of the Church. He is a man of unreasonable hopes and expectations, who takes seriously, for himself and others, the injunction to be perfect as the heavenly Father is."

He said that priests must be good men, men who provide for their physical and emotional health. They cannot hide from life. They need affection. Their priesthood must be fed by "an inner silence, a spiritual tranquility, public and private prayer and an abiding joy. Without prejudice to the important social mission of the Church, the basic thrust of our efforts as priests must be spiritual."

During that homily Cardinal Bernardin spoke of his predecessor, Cardinal Cody: "I was four years old when the Cardinal became a priest and he was Archbishop of Chicago longer than I have been a bishop. Thus we are men of different generations and different experiences of Church and episcopal ministry.

"I was saddened by the pain, suffering and conflict that seemed to cloud his final years. He was called to leadership in the Church during years of unprecedented change and turmoil. The achievements of his fifty years of priesthood are real and lasting. By any objective measure, Cardinal Cody did many good things for Chicago which make my work easier. If any hard feelings, bitterness or anger —toward the Cardinal or among yourselves—remain in your hearts for any reason, tonight is the night to cast off the burden and purify your hearts."

He concluded: "You will know me as a friend, fellow priest and bishop. You will know also that I love you. For I am Joseph, your brother!"

He echoed that statement when he addressed a

distinguished Chicagoland Jewish audience, telling his Jewish neighbors: "I am Joseph, your brother!"

In that close relationship Cardinal Bernardin sees a consistent expression of his feeling about all women and men, clerical and lay. He adheres to Catholic Church positions on ordination, seeing it as a possibility only for men. Yet women occupy an important position in his life, beginning with Mary the mother of Christ Jesus, and including his own mother Maria, women religious and women in the laity.

Of course there is something special in his view of the priesthood. He shares many of his most private hours with priests, who work closely with him, who share his residence with him. He is comfortable with priests, but he is by no means uncomfortable with others. Father James Roache became aware of this long before he was invited to live in the Cardinal's residence in Chicago.

In the early 1970s Father Roache was one of two press officers serving at national meetings of the bishops. One of the first things he noticed about Bishop Bernardin in those days was that he had time for people, that he was aware of newcomers, such as a press officer. He was clear-minded, highly regarded by his peers, ready to listen to others and accept ideas. He was kind. He was at home with everyone.

Chapter Ten

CHICAGO'S Presbyteral Senate illustrates the powerful cooperation that exists between ordained priests and ordained permanent deacons. The Archdiocese of Chicago led the country in developing the permanent diaconate program after Vatican Council II. Just a day after his formal installation as the Archbishop of Chicago, Joseph Bernardin delivered the homily at an evening prayer service with permanent deacons and their wives in Holy Name Cathedral.

He said: "There are over 400 deacons in the archdiocese. Many large dioceses in this country do not even have 400 priests. How fortunate we are. Too many deacons? That is certainly not my thinking. I bless the memory of Cardinal Cody for his openness and foresight in encouraging the growth of the permanent diaconate. Because you come from all walks of life, from all parts of the city and suburbs, from many different ethnic and racial backgrounds, including numbers of black and Hispanic deacons, you manifest the catholicity of the Church in a unique way."

Cardinal Bernardin recalled that much of today's talk in the Church would be quite a mystery to anyone who had been isolated since before the Second Vatican Council. There's a lot of conversation today about Church ministry and ministries that could not have taken place with the same meaning in relatively recent days. Protestants had ministers; Catholics had priests. So be it. The diaconate was simply one step in a seminarian's experience as he moved toward priestly ordination. Then the Council put new emphasis on the doctrine that through Baptism all become part of a holy priesthood, that Jesus is the high priest and all members of the Church should make his priesthood evident everywhere by celebrating the sacraments and engaging in Christian service. Dioceses moved to restore the ministry of permanent deacons.

And so, Cardinal Bernardin said in Holy Name Cathedral: "You permanent deacons act both as 'ministers' in a strict sense and as secular lay persons in the world. While you are truly ordained into the first of the three orders of the hierarchy, making you important co-workers with bishops and priests, your secular employment and family life make you a bridge between priests and religious who labor full-time in the Church and lay leaders whose Christian lives are lived almost exclusively in the secular world. Through you the Church is being built up and strengthened in a new way."

Their wives share much of the preparation of married permanent deacons because they are called upon to share the burdens and satisfactions of Christian family life and the particular demands of the Christian community. Those precise burdens and satisfactions are not experienced by Cardinal Bernardin or any of his priests. More than one woman has speculated on what it would mean to be married to an archbishop if the Church were to permit it. Reporters who interview laicized priests who later married usually overlook an interview with their wives, who might have some thoughts of their own. Family life is demanding on all caring wives and husbands, whatever the work of their spouses may be.

A Protestant woman once asked me, with a chuckle: "Do you know what's wrong with Cardinal Cody?" I admitted that I hadn't thought much about it at the time. "There's no Mrs. Cody!" said my friend. Bishops who wonder how to get twenty-five hours of preaching, presiding, writing, signing, speaking, being interviewed, studying, researching, examining budgets, driving to Confirmations, attending dinners, attending breakfasts, attending luncheons, reading documents, reviewing decisions that require approval, exercising, talking on the telephone and of course celebrating the sacraments and praying, into twenty-four hours of a day may have some thoughts of their own about my friend's wisecrack.

Religious men and women can understand those thoughts of busy bishops because they are often overworked themselves. As Cardinal Bernardin observed when he spoke to them on the morning of his second full day as Archbishop of Chicago, they spend their energies in forms of pastoral service that often are neither noticed nor appreciated. Yet their influence is wide and lasting.

The Cardinal spoke of Mary's visit to her cousin Elizabeth and of Elizabeth's joy in her kinship of the Savior who is to be born. "The fact that both are with child draws our attention to femininity, womanhood and of course maternity," said the new Archbishop of Chicago. Other passages in the Bible narrative focus upon the men in their lives—Zecheriah, who was the father of John the Baptist, and Joseph, the foster father of Jesus.

"These four great biblical figures are, of course, exemplars for all who seek to love and serve God," Cardinal Bernardin told the religious. "In a special way, however, I believe they tell us much that is important for the consecrated, vowed lives of those who have committed themselves to the service of the Lord as sisters and brothers. Mary and Elizabeth, Joseph and Zecheriah were all called to say yes to his or her vocation."

He went on to say that his listeners "have said yes to the Lord and his call to poverty, chastity and obedience. You have gone against the current of the times that stresses self-fulfillment to the point of narcissism." He did not agree with those who say that the permanent vows of religious violate human dignity and freedom, seeing them as freely-accepted gifts.

He said: "In the years since the Council every form of Christian ministry has been analyzed by some in terms of secular understanding. Such analyses can have value, but only if carried on in the framework established by faith itself. It is not secular wisdom which is the judge of faith, but faith which ultimately judges secular wisdom."

He continued: "Religious life, too, has sought renewed self-understanding in these years. Be assured that your effort to rediscover yourselves, your common meaning, your spirituality, has taken place within a similar effort by the whole Church. As the Church's effort has centered on rediscovering the revelation that is Jesus along with the experience he communicated to the apostles, yours also must center on the same experience of Christ, as well as on what was special to the founders and foundresses of your communities. This is the work of a lifetime, to be embraced fully and lovingly."

Cardinal Bernardin asked the religious men and women to work toward the elimination of all ethnic and racial prejudice, a plea that he took to all residents of Chicago during the 1983 mayoral election which found a black Protestant Democrat facing a white Jewish Republican candidate. He urged the religious to embrace more members of the Hispanic and black communites "so that you can be enriched by their many spiritual gifts." He sought their help in breaking down divisions between groups and classes, to speak out for the poor and powerless, to press for human development and authentic liberation.

Years before he had told Ursuline Sisters during a workshop in Cleveland that the religious life is marked by specific charisms.

"Whatever else is involved," he said in 1977, "the definition of a religious as prophet and witness comes first." He also said: "The impact of this witness must never be swallowed up in a secularism that is antithetical to the resurrected life to which you are called to bear witness. Some of our newer life styles do not belie the witness of religious to those who believe deeply and have the power to put things into proper perspective, but they can cause a lot of confusion for those who are simpler and are just not getting the prophetic message any more." In the first burst of enthusiasm for renewal, he said, there was sometimes a mistaken downgrading of some vital apostolates, such as teaching. He repeated the call of the bishops in their collective pastoral letter "To Teach as Jesus Did" to make Catholic schools "instruments for proclaiming the Gospel message, building up a faith community and preparing persons for service to others."

He cautioned that involvement in the pastoral life of a diocese carries responsibilities with it. He told the sisters that "when you project yourselves into the pastoral ministry, you are no longer alone; your own personal interests as religious (no matter how legitimate or necessary they might be) are not the only factor to be considered.

"You must also take into account the good of the local Church you are serving. You must, therefore, work very closely with the local Church, especially the bishop as its chief pastor. The discernment process now so popular in many religious congregations can lead you astray unless it is carried on within those established structures of the Church through which the Spirit works."

He addressed another concern of religious during a homily for the sesquicentennial Mass of the Sisters of Mercy, Cincinnati Province, in December of 1981, calling upon the sisters to carry out their work "precisely as religious."

Cardinal Bernardin is associated daily with religious. There are the Felician Sisters who staff the stately Queen Anne home that Chicago's first archbishop, Patrick A. Feehan, erected. There are the Little Sisters of the Poor who staff the home in which his mother lives, and which the Cardinal visits daily when he's in town. There are more than 300 brothers and nearly 5,000 sisters in the Archdiocese of Chicago.

Well enough. The Cardinal embraces clergy and religious as Joseph their brother. Most of them are ready to respond with an affectionate hug. A few sisters have grumbled privately about his failure to defy the Pope and the Church on that touchy matter of ordination for women, but they're not prepared to give up either their affection for the Cardinal or their personal convictions. After all, they acknowledge, not even Rome was built in a day.

Chapter Eleven

COLUMNISTS, commentators and editorial writers puckered their brows and headed for their typewriters some time back when it was reported that school children had little interest in becoming President of the United States. Somebody had committed another survey, this one on youngsters to find out what they'd like to be, and what they'd just as soon avoid, when they grew up.

It was found that they had little desire to live in the White House. Boys and girls agreed that the job was too tough, that it had more drawbacks than advantages as far as they could see and that they'd rather do something else—almost anything else. The gossip of history includes anecdotes about men who did not want to be Pope, who accepted election reluctantly, out of a sense of duty that could not be ignored.

Those cautious children probably had seen enough television news shows to know what happens to a President after the inaugural parade is over, after the bands have packed their instruments and the banners have been taken down. The complaints begin. Some come from the opposition party but many come from the President's own political household. Newspaper cartoonists go to work on the President, editorialists take aim, the letters-to-the-editor become grim and abusive, foreign leaders make speeches of hearty denunciation and privacy becomes unaffordable on the President's salary.

The mentally disturbed keep the President in their anxious thoughts and once in a while one of them thinks about visiting a firearms dealer. So maybe those children who

99

decided quite early that the presidency wasn't for them, and the otherwise ambitious politicians who didn't want to be President, the intelligent and dedicated men who'd just as soon let somebody else be Pope, were not as peculiar in their views as it might seem. Not everyone is ready to pay the price that accompanies power.

You'd think that once elected Pope you would be free to enjoy the position and the honor, to say nothing of the palaces and chartered airplanes. It does not work that way. The Pope starts out with some millions of instant critics who believe that any Pope, no matter how attractive personally, is the personification of all that was wrong in Babylon and is the enemy of the Lord himself. The more extravagant the delusion the more tenacious its appeal seems to be in some quarters, with some groups and individuals.

Then there are the anxieties among those who serve the Pope in his own administrative structures, the criticisms that come from Catholics who think that he's moving too quickly or too slowly, the shoulder-shrugging from some who think that a Pope is necessary but not necessarily relevant. And not even the Pope, known to Catholics as the vicar of Jesus Christ, is any more immune to violence than Jesus was.

Interior strength helps some Presidents and Popes to serve with what the world thinks of as greatness, a quality to be respected and emulated. Abraham Lincoln and George Washington, St. Peter and John XXIII, were perceived in this way during their own lifetimes. The same kind of strength contributes to the making of all successful church leaders, whether they're priests helping alcoholics to rebuild their lives, sisters meeting ugly problems of poverty right on the scene or bishops contributing to an atmosphere of spiritual growth in the community. If anything is absolutely dependable it is the fact that there will be opposition and discontent, that sincerity alone is not enough.

Cardinal Bernardin was received with almost unanimous delight when he moved to Chicago, but there were some who muttered that the new archbishop was getting entirely too much time on television and too many column inches in the press. The reception he received from enthusiastic priests, religious, deacons and laity was spontaneous and geniune. Universal? Well, almost, but there's a touch of grumpiness everywhere and Cardinal Bernardin has no protection from the unsatisfied. There aren't many of them, and some who disagree with him on one part of his job support him in the rest.

Great crowds turned out in Cincinnati to show their affection and to let him know how greatly they valued his decade there. Among them were a couple of priests who told visitors that they might still see as much of Archbishop Bernardin as they had when he lived among them in Ohio. "His bags were always packed," one said. "He came home in order to pick up a fresh bag and head out again." Some Vatican workers have said the same thing about the Pope. It is not true literally, and it doesn't even have a lot of truth in it, but it shows that not even the overachiever can satisfy everybody.

Cardinal Bernardin's relations with clergy and religious have been excellent. Even the Chicagoland priests who told friends that they'd have to wait and see how he worked out after he'd been here a while were among the almost instantaneous enthusiasts. Ecclesiastical muggers were out, huggers were in.

Only about six months after he took over the Archdiocese of Chicago, some of the best-known organized critics of his predecessor were looking toward new directions.

By April 1983 the Association of Chicago Priests, known as the ACP, spent most of a two-hour meeting to explore its future. By that time the ACP had a membership of nearly 475 priests, deacons and resigned priests. It had worked for years to try to encourage a different course for Cardinal Cody; finally it charted a head-on collision course that included active campaigning to have Cardinal Cody replaced.

In 1971 the ACP voted, 144 to 126, to censure Cardinal Cody and his auxiliary bishops for what it called "their silence" during a spring meeting of the National Conference of Catholic Bishops in Detroit. A resolution accused the Chicago bishops of failing to raise "some voice for openness to the strong, documented call of American priests for new forms of priestly life and ministry."

There was shock among Catholics everywhere. Nobody in Chicago could remember anything like it. Five auxiliaries were present at the meeting. Their spokesman was Bishop William E. McManus, who was to become the Bishop of Fort Wayne and South Bend in Indiana and chairman of the board of Our Sunday Visitor in Huntington, Ind. In response to the 1971 ACP censure he said this: "Our purpose is to set the record straight for the priests of the Archdiocese and also for the general public who have read the controversial accusations and perhaps presume there is guilt if the charges are not responded to forcefully." Cardinal Cody stayed away from the meeting "so as to express a sadness at the disunity and fragmentation presented in your document as distributed and publicized.'' He said, as he often did in other circumstances, that the presence of the Archbishop anywhere should always be seen as a sign of unity.

The action was unprecedented, and although it was approved by only 144 votes in an Archdiocese that had more than 2,300 priests, it attracted wide attention and created a lasting rift. In addition to Bishop McManus, the auxiliaries included in the censure were Bishops Nevin W. Hayes, O.Carm., and Alfred L. Abramowicz, who were still auxiliaries when Cardinal Bernardin reached Chicago; Thomas J. Grady, who became Bishop of Orlando in Florida, and Michael R. Dempsey, widely admired as a spokesman for the poor, who later died.

A year earlier the Association of Chicago Priests, during a meeting in Cicero, asked for an end to the traditional law of celibacy and asked for limited tenure in office for pastors. The ACP didn't stop with the adoption of resolutions, but showed its early and lasting understanding of communications, especially that part of it that's loosely called public relations, by sharing its decision with Pope Paul VI, Cardinal Cody, the National Conference of Catholic Bishops and the National Federation of Priests' Councils.

Cardinal Cody, who in those days had more to say publicly about ACP actions than he did in later years, when he tended to ignore the association, had this to say: ''Newspaper accounts describing a vote taken at a meeting of the priests' association on the question of optional celibacy pointed out that the result of the vote was 398 for optional celibacy and 184 against changing the Church's existing legislation on celibacy. What they failed to point

out is that in the Archdiocese of Chicago there are some
3,000 [sic] priests. While the vote that was taken is of
importance in showing the mood of the priests who had
gathered for this meeting, it would perhaps be an exaggera-
tion to extend this sentiment to those who would not
attend a meeting of this nature.

"Moreover, the question of celibacy is not merely a local
issue, nor one of interest only to priests. It must be seen in
the context of a worldwide practice for priests of the Latin
rite; it must be evaluated in terms of its significance to the
total People of God. The voice of the laity is of equal
importance in any debate on this issue.

"Likewise the question on tenure of the pastoral office
is one which involves the laity and cannot be changed except through a possible revision of canon law. Certainly we
all understand the feelings of our priests in these changing
times. We anguish with them in the critical decisions they
are facing, but we must state clearly that we stand with the
Holy Father and the bishops of the United States in
upholding the tradition of a celibate clergy."

That 1970 Cicero meeting and the 1971 censure meeting,
which was held at Resurrection Parish, signaled the opening of a public battle which was to inflame the Church in
Chicago for years to come and ultimately to cause heavy
setbacks for Cardinal Cody. But at the time the first flares
zoomed into the ecclesial sky, Cardinal Cody had the sym-
pathy and support of virtually the entire episcopacy in the
United States. He had the Holy See substantially on his
side and was backed by the laity to a large degree.

Some of the auxiliary bishops who were rapped in the
censure vote were popular, even beloved figures. It didn't
surprise the public at large that members of the hierarchy

supported the Pope's position on celibacy, nor was it a surprise to many that auxiliary bishops did not routinely
disagree with their ordinary in public. Later, some of the
ACP members acknowledged that they might have been
too quick to censure the auxiliaries or even the Cardinal
himself.

Certainly the Cardinal thought they were too quick and
he never forgot. It was the end of his feelings of pride,
which he described with these words during a 1967 plenary
session of the Association of Chicago Priests: "I believe
the priests' association of Chicago meets the problems and
tries to find a solution, and this is the best way in the spirit
of the Second Vatican Council." Father Raymond E.
Goedert, then chairman of the ACP coordinating committee and later an influential pastor, said that the ACP was
"bringing the democratic spirit into the Church—and that
is not rebellion."

By 1971 almost 80 percent of the priests voted by mail to
ratify a constitution for a new Presbyteral Senate. The ten-
page document had been drafted by a 51-member committee appointed by Cardinal Cody. Before long Father
Goedert was president of the Senate, and in 1974 he included some good news and some bad news in his
annual report. He thought a survey had helped the Senate
to set its own priorities, but said: "I am afraid we still have
a long way to go before the relationship of the Senate to
the priests at large and to the Cardinal is all that it should
be. There is no doubt about it, the experience of collegial
decision making is still a very new one for all of us and it
will take years, if not decades, for bishops and priests to
adjust to these unfamiliar roles." His report was made to
the third annual meeting of the full presbyterate.

Father Goedert said: "The Church is in transition now, and I am not about to walk away from her because the going is rough. Shifting gears from an authoritarian, monarchical structure to one in which responsibility is truly shared is no easier than for a diesel to climb a mountain. But the power is there—in the Holy Spirit, and I know that one day the Church will attain the transformation we so earnestly seek."

In 1971 the Senate's first president, Father Thomas J. Murphy, said the organization was unique. He said there were as many priests in the Chicago Senate as there were in some U.S. dioceses. There were so many priests, in fact, that it was almost impossible to get them all together in one place at one time and it was difficult, maybe impossible, to get unanimous agreement on controversial questions. Just how much the fact of bigness influenced the growing problems will be debated for a long time. How Cardinal Cody and his priests responded to the problems had something to do with the reception that Cardinal Cody's successor received. How that response lasted, developed, helped shape new attitudes, had more to do with Cardinal Bernardin than with anyone who had gone before.

The Senate became the "official" organization of priests during the latter Cody years and the ACP became the "unofficial" organization of priests and others in the Archdiocese. Relations between the Archbishop and both organizations were strained at times, but there was open hostility between Cardinal Cody and the ACP.

By 1977 the ACP had sent a letter to Pope John Paul II outlining grievances against Cardinal Cody. Father Joseph J. O'Brien, who was ACP chairman at the time, would not talk publicly about the contents of the hand-delivered letter. Cardinal Cody had nothing to say about the letter. He knew that many Chicagoans had written to the Pope and to the Apostolic Delegate, beginning during the pontificate of Paul VI, to object to his administration of the Archdiocese. He had denied reports that the Vatican had sought to lure him away from Chicago with an offer of an impressive post in Rome.

During the same period Paul Palmer, a Chicago layman representing a group called Save Our Shrine, said that he and another member of his organization had called on Sebastiano Cardinal Baggio, then prefect of the Congregation for Bishops, to seek help in reopening Sacred Heart Church after it had been closed by Cardinal Cody. Cardinal Bernardin later reopened the shrine, but for Cardinal Cody the episode was one of several that made his declining years a time of defensive response to various accusations.

After Cardinal Cody replaced Father James Roache, his secretary of communications, with a new lay director of communications, there was additional turmoil in the press. Father Roache, respected by his peers, was soon elected president of the Presbyteral Senate. He was to become Cardinal Bernardin's administrative assistant and to share his residence.

Picketing of Cardinal Cody's residence for one reason or another became almost routine. A sign was posted marking it as "private property" to keep protestors off the lawn and out of the driveway. Cardinal Cody was generally quietly defiant, saying little to the protestors but reminding his public that "in the law of the Catholic Church, in each diocese there is but one authority—the ordinary."

The law was in a process of change even then, and much

that was to become official in the revised Code of Canon Law was anticipated in practice in many places, including Chicago. But Cardinal Cody was uncertain about the desirability of all of the changes and he knew quite clearly what the law said.

Once as we were talking in the reception room of his residence I mentioned a contested issue and said that I thought it was referred to in canon law. "It is not in canon law," he told me, and then gave me the precise place to find it in other Church documentation.

While Cardinal Bernardin was in Rome to receive his red hat on February 2, 1983, Catholics everywhere were talking about the promulgation of a new Code of Canon Law by Pope John Paul II on January 25. The revisions caused no concerns for Cardinal Bernardin, who was among those pleasantly anticipating them. Father Robert C. Becker of the Chicago Metropolitan Tribunal was president of the Canon Law Society of America when the new code was published. When I asked him about it he said that the "musts" are greatly reduced. "It is almost as though somebody took seriously the idea that the Church should be governed by the Gospel of love, that the Church should state the essential principles and let people work out the details." He explained further that the old law saw the bishop as all-knowing, except in some narrowly defined areas. "The revised law turns that inside out. It presumes a broad level of intense consultation."

Both the law and the style changed after Cardinal Bernardin took over. He continued his practice, which was not new to him in either Washington or Cincinnati, of consulting widely. Some felt, in Washington and Cincinnati, that he could consult too widely at times, that the creation of committees did not necessarily lead to quick or even skilled solutions to problems. But how else does one person carry out the several dozen distinct tasks that appear on the job description of the head of a major diocese? Members of the Presbyteral Senate asked themselves what kind of man Cardinal Cody's successor should be. The Cardinal was expected to retire on his 75th birthday, Dec. 24, 1982. He died before that retirement date.

Priests who speculated on his successor looked for "humanness" along with "warmth, openness, acceptance, even vulnerability," said Father Thomas Healy, the Senate president in mid-1982. "The senators reflected the presbyterate's need for shepherding, healing and reconciling, the need for someone to bring us—priests and laity—together. The shepherd should be one who shares responsibility, delegates authority and trusts a collegial Vatican II Church."

As someone observed later, Father Healy might have been talking about Cardinal Bernardin.

Chapter Twelve

CARDINAL Bernardin inherited a polarized and fragmented Church, but one that remained powerful in many respects. Many Chicagoland priests had openly opposed Cardinal Cody. Others quietly opposed him, withdrawing as far as they could from close association with "downtown," the Archdiocesan Administrative Center at 155 East Superior Street, not far from Chicago's famed water tower and just a short walk from Holy Name Cathedral. Chicago was a leader in significant areas during the Cody years, notably in liturgy.

Father Daniel Coughlin, director of the Office for Divine Worship, worked with a talented staff and helped develop an awareness of liturgical developments throughout the Archdiocese. Someone quipped that bishops traveled to Chicago from all over the United States for Cardinal Cody's funeral, many of them thinking it would be nice to become the Archbishop of Chicago, but that they departed, following the liturgy, thinking that it would be great to be the rector of Holy Name Cathedral. It was Cardinal Cody, of course, who encouraged growth in the liturgy and in other major areas of Church life.

The polarization and fragmentation harmed a whole generation of Chicagoland Catholics, causing a withdrawal from the sense of identity that had given the Church of Chicago a specific grandeur, a feeling among priests and religious that it was the place to be.

Some time earlier, when I was a trustee of St. Mary's University and Seminary in Baltimore, I stopped to talk with a young man on his way to the priesthood. He told me that he was from Chicago and I congratulated him on his years ahead in his hometown. "I'm not going to be in Chicago," he said. I asked him where he would serve. "I don't know yet, but I don't want to be a priest in Chicago because of the tensions there." Those tensions had a way of causing many priests and religious to concentrate almost entirely on parish life, where they developed some outstanding programs.

There was an inevitable loss, though, of the feeling, especially among the laity in those parishes, of what it means to be an active part of the universal Church, of a Church that is not defined exclusively by the boundaries of a parish.

Cardinal Cody was concerned with every detail of management, although nobody could possibly keep up with all of the details in an archdiocese of some 450 parishes and numerous institutions. One pastor told me of receiving a telephone call from Cardinal Cody at 11 o'clock at night. He wondered whether he might be getting an answer to a personal request he'd submitted some time before. "Father," he recalled the Cardinal saying to him over the phone, "I've been sitting here reading the list of building permits and find that you've done some remodeling; I don't recall that you obtained permission for that." The astonished pastor explained that the remodeling was in parish property that had been leased for use by another agency, and he was off the hook.

Cardinal Cody had an eye for details, the kind of attention to such things that has been attributed to President Jimmy Carter, and it sometimes was a substitute for delegation of authority. Cardinal Cody sometimes took a literal view of the corporation sole, the legal instrument that placed most of the property of the Archdiocese under the control of the Ordinary, the Archbishop. He gave little authority to his Finance Committee, on which I served a couple of terms.

Along with the troublesome aspects of confrontation and alienation, Cardinal Bernardin inherited an Archdiocese that was financially sound but which operated at a deficit. The first financial report published by Cardinal Bernardin in *The Chicago Catholic* showed that during the previous fiscal year expenses exceeded income, other than from security investments, by $2.6 million. Cumulative operating deficits for the decade beginning in 1972 were listed at $29 million.

The report also showed assets of considerably more than two billion dollars as of June 30, 1982. The precise figure was $2,278,174,000. Much of that represented real estate that, unlike commercial real estate assets, operates year after year at a loss and is, in fact, a drain on finances. Owning a church building or a rectory is not the equivalent of owning a supermarket or an apartment house. But the report listed security investments at $149,745,000 at market value.

By way of comparison with the world of commerce, a newspaper industry analyst said that his incomplete calculations put the value of the Chicago *Sun-Times* at "around $250,000,000 or so." The analyst, John Morton of the Wall Street firm of Lynch, Jones & Ryan, was quoted in *The New York Times* after it was announced that Field Enterprises had decided to sell the *Sun-Times* and other properties. Cardinal Bernardin appointed a blue ribbon Audit Committee of community leaders and made it clear that he would have an open and accountable administration. The financial concerns facing him were formidable. It takes a lot of money to keep the Church of Chicago going, to subsidize education, to provide services to the needy, the divorced, minorities, parishes in poverty areas and to meet scores of urgent needs—some of them new and impossible to anticipate.

Cardinal Cody shared with Cardinal Bernardin a deep love for the Catholic Church, but comparisons are awkward. Sometimes they hardly seem reasonable. Cardinal Bernardin can readily be compared with his predecessor as president of the National Conference of Catholic Bishops, John Cardinal Dearden, former Archbishop of Detroit. He can be compared easily with John Cardinal Krol of Philadelphia, who succeeded him as president.

It is more of a challenge to try to compare him with Cardinal Cody, who wasn't entirely convinced of the value of national conferences of bishops. Yet some understanding of the ways of Cardinals Cody and Bernardin, including their differences, is necessary in recognizing the impact of Cardinal Bernardin on a troubled Church of Chicago.

Cardinal Cody sometimes answered his critics but more often he ignored them. He promoted some of them. He insisted that his way was the only correct way and believed that history would prove him right. Scores of times he talked with me about his plans to write his autobiography and said that it would "set some people on their ears." He told me that he wanted me to spend some time with him in the quiet atmosphere he could find at St. Mary of the Lake Seminary in Mundelein, working with him to get started on the book.

Nothing that I've written about his views or his actions

violates a confidence. He was quick, sometimes too quick perhaps, in saying what he thought. He did not care who knew what he thought. I didn't win many arguments with him, but he always listened. The arguments I won usually concerned his decision to speak out bluntly on a controversial question when I thought that everybody's interests, especially his, would be served best by a period of reflection and the use of softer tones.

After I told a group of journalists what Cardinal Cody thought about the media, and especially the Catholic press, one priest chided me for including what he perceived to be negative comments. I was able to assure him that I had not presented to that group of journalists any views of Cardinal Cody that the Cardinal had not himself put on the record. He was outspoken in criticism of the media, and that included criticism of his own newspaper from time to time. He felt that he was right and he did not mind being quoted as long as the quotation was accurate. His likes and dislikes were equally strong and clear.

His successor as Archbishop of Chicago is also clear and outspoken, but his goals and background are not the same. He has a different response to the pull toward an essentially monarchical episcopacy on the one hand or an essentially pastoral episcopacy on the other. The dilemma is not unlike one that is faced throughout the Church, beginning in the Holy See. By no means all of the bureaucracy of the Church is concerned with self protection, including the preservation of power and privilege.

The institutional Church operates at many levels. The parish is institutional in essential respects. How else would buildings be maintained, heat provided, bills paid, bulletins printed, projects funded, salaries covered, educational programs carried out, the particular needs of the poor and the elderly and the young addressed? The scale is different in the diocese, but the institutional requirements are curiously similar to those of the parish or those of the Holy See.

It is a frequent wry observation that those who object to anything institutional usually begin by forming a committee, the very foundation of all institutional activity. Others turn to institutional courts to complain about institutional charities. Government is primarily institutional, lacking the vital spiritual impetus that is the very reason for an institutional Church.

Almost everyone in the Church hailed the Second Vatican Council and the institutional growth that it set in motion. The Church of Chicago was not alone in creating new agencies to meet the expectations growing out of Vatican II. Offices and agencies were created or expanded to meet new concerns, ranging from homosexuality and divorce to social justice and Charismatic renewal.

The Roman Curia grew just as dioceses and parishes grew in meeting institutional expectations, whether for school boards and parish councils or for interfaith bureaus. The key element in each case is pastoral. If the school board, parish council, interfaith agency and pontifical commission see their work as being related directly to the service of the Lord and the Lord's people, the institution avoids institutionalism.

Some of the institutions take on democratic forms, but the Catholic Church is not a democracy. A pastor has defined responsibilities in a parish, even though he reaches out widely for consultation and uses democratic procedures effectively. An ordinary remains responsible for some decisions, even if they are offered to him by a committee that has organized itself democratically.

The uses of democratic procedures come quite naturally to most Americans, but they do not predominate throughout the world. The Holy See is not a democracy. Pope John Paul II has never lived in a democracy that depends upon free elections and individual rights. He has never lived in a capitalistic society. He is able to make use of democratic mechanisms and of capitalistic enterprises, but the Holy See has never operated along the lines of an American town meeting and has little in common, structurally, with the U.S. federal government. Final authority rests with the Pope.

Consultation is encouraged by Pope John Paul II, who shares Cardinal Bernardin's quality of being a good listener. There is substantial authority for the structure of Church government to be found in tradition and Scripture, but much of the institutional tradition has roots in a history that pre-dates the nation state and that includes the era of the absolute monarch.

Relating that tradition with the growth of individual initiative and decision-making by majority vote is part of the challenge of bishops, including Cardinal Bernardin. It is visible in his habit of consultation, but nobody doubts who takes responsibility for final decisions of any consequence.

Democracy works from the bottom up; hierarchy works from the top down. Cardinal Bernardin manages to make both approaches work up, down and across, like a successful crossword puzzle. This effort is closely related to the concept of a universal Church that includes and somehow extends the local Church. This might be a dilemma to some, but to Cardinal Bernardin it is not. It is the way things are and he always moves to make the best use of existing structures, even while trying to improve them.

The late John Cardinal Wright was conscious of this, as he moved his way from being an archbishop's secretary to being an auxiliary bishop, then an ordinary and finally the prefect of the Sacred Congregation for the Clergy. He understood the enormous variation in traditions and expectations within local Catholic Churches and the necessity of bringing to that variety a feeling of unity in the universal Church.

This is not a concern unique to Chicago. Cardinal Wright had great respect for the Church in Poland, often observing that there was no shortage of young men interested in the priesthood in that country. He thought that American Catholics in many ways had things too easy, that the attractions of secularism were too subtle and too pronounced. Yet he knew about the values of pride in the local Church, even when he was reminded of it in an awkward way.

The first year after he stepped aside as the Bishop of Pittsburgh and moved to his new post in Rome he returned to Washington to attend the annual meeting of the National Conference of Catholic Bishops. Everyone there was a friend. Many were old and intimate friends. But he discovered that he, the former Bishop of Pittsburgh, was now an outsider at the meeting of the national episcopacy. He had become a Roman, a member of the Curia, the head of a congregation serving the Holy See.

His old friends at home no longer saw him as a part of their conference and as we sat talking quietly in the hotel lobby he acknowledged to me that they were right. He often returned to the United States after that, but not as an American bishop. The weaving together of different views and expectations calls for the kind of skill that may come more or less naturally to Cardinal Bernardin, son of a talented mother whose sewing skills were the envy of many.

Like Cardinal Wright, Cardinal Bernardin has admired the Church and people in Poland. When he was president of the U.S. episcopal conference he visited Poland. He was accompanied by his successor as general secretary of the conference, the late Bishop James Rausch, and others. Although the powerful Marian influence in the life of Polish Catholics is admirable, it probably does not correspond precisely to Cardinal Bernardin's intense focus upon Jesus Christ. His devotion to Mary is not diminished by that focus.

In Cincinnati he was heard on the radio leading the recitation of the Rosary, a recitation that continues to inspire many who listen to it on cassettes. He knows the strengths of the Church in Poland, sees evidence of that strength among the numerous Polish Catholics in Chicago and follows it as it manifests in the person of the Pope.

Cardinal Bernardin was well known to fellow churchmen in various parts of the world through his intense work in the Synod of Bishops and his leadership of the National Conference of Catholic Bishops. He's well liked even where he is not personally known.

Robert Nowell, author of several books about Catholic life and London-based correspondent for the National Catholic News Service, told me that Cardinal Bernardin is seen in Britain as a "sort of Derek Worlock of American bishops." Archbishop Worlock of Liverpool, born in 1920, is personally attractive to English Catholics, is well known at the Holy See and is noted for vigorous leadership. He was a secretary to English bishops at the outset of the Second Vatican Council and became a bishop in October 1965.

Robert Nowell said that Cardinal Bernardin is seen by Europeans as "cool, capable, one who finds solutions, one who does his homework. He's held in great affection. Basil Hume [the Cardinal Archbishop of Westminster] likes him a lot. He's not seen as the kind of intellectual pioneer who sometimes makes life exciting, but he's respected for his skills in other areas. He is highly regarded both for his thinking and for his administrative skills."

His administrative skills are well known and have been written about frequently. His diplomatic skills are equally impressive. They are applied more or less constantly, even unconsciously, and nothing can be more diplomatic than that. During all of the tugs for his time and attention at the outset of his life in Chicago he was occupied with the almost overwhelming job of putting together a collective pastoral letter on war and peace issues, one that would not simply be acceptable to Catholics of different political persuasions but one of power and movement. That required him to meet with leaders of the European hierarchy, who already respected him and felt affection for him.

He and his associates managed to bring them together, to keep the center of attention on the central moral and ethical concerns that had to be faced by Christians addressing a largely non-Christian world. It is his worldview that has impressed many whose early thought of him was cautious. His worldview has been one of the elements helping him to draw local views together and to enlarge upon them. It has had a part in his appeal to the fragmented elements of the Catholic Church in Chicagoland.

One of the first men to meet with him after he began his Chicago duties was Viatorian Father John E. Linnan, president of the Catholic Theological Union in Chicago. This has been described as the largest Roman Catholic school of ministry on the North American continent, but it was out of favor with Cardinal Cody.

Cardinal Cody was restrained in his view of the divinity school because it trained many women for Church ministry short of ordination. It teaches only graduate students, is supported by nearly two dozen religious orders and has no formal affiliation with the Archdiocese of Chicago. Father Linnan was impressed by his conversation with Cardinal Bernardin, who visited the Catholic Theological Union in the spring of 1983.

While I was interviewing Father Linnan in his office he asked a question: "Can we have a genuine North American Roman Catholic Church that's different from a Latin American or African or Japanese Roman Catholic Church?" His doctorate at Louvain grew out of a study of John Henry Cardinal Newman, so it was natural for him to say: "Newman concluded that the Church is not a gathering of believers, but a community of believers that can communicate grace. The Church itself is a sacrament. Newman asked himself where, in the multiplicity of community, is Church. He studied the fourth century Arians and decided there had to be a principle of authority. After that, Newman asked himself how the Church should deal with authority in a time of change. How do we justify development in worship and dogma?"

Certainly he and Cardinal Bernardin had a lot to talk about, especially because the Catholic Theological Union tries to meet the special, sometimes touchy, cultural and spiritual anxieties of local Churches within the universal Church. It also has developed a somewhat corresponding concern for meeting the expectations and requirements of inner city parishes as parts of a larger local Church, increasingly suburban and middle class.

Cardinal Bernardin talks with men and women who speak for each of the many concerns that can result in fragmentation or unity. His tilt is clearly toward unity and it did not take long for results of that tilt to become evident in a broader popular commitment to catholicity in Christ's Church. He achieved these gains in the course of supporting without any evasion the leadership of the Pope. It was an accomplishment that could scarcely have been expected a couple of years earlier, one that disarmed most of his potential critics and brought them home.

Chapter Thirteen

RIGHT after I became editor of Chicago's archdiocesan newspaper late in 1976 I received a call from one of Cardinal Cody's secretaries. She knew that I was living temporarily in a hotel room that was a bit grandly known as an efficiency apartment, waiting for school terms to end back in suburban Washington before moving my family. The Cardinal, she said, wanted me to have a private telephone line installed in the hotel room and to equip it with an answering machine capable of recording lengthy messages in my absence.

After that I never knew when the telephone would ring, with Cardinal Cody on the line asking a question or offering a comment on something in the news. He usually made the calls himself and as soon as the phone was answered he began speaking, without any preliminaries.

After the family joined me I had to warn each person at home that if a caller simply began talking it was likely to be His Eminence. Cardinal Cody was right at home with every instrument of communication and apparently spent much of his time tracking down information or sharing ideas on the telephone.

Right beside my bedroom phone at home I set up a miniature library that included the *Official Directory of the Archdiocese of Chicago*, the *Annuario Pontificio* published in Vatican City, the *Official Catholic Directory* published by Kenedy and giving detailed information about all dioceses in the United States, the *Catholic Almanac*, the *Catholic Press Directory* and various other reference works. I kept copies of the archdiocesan newspaper and, of course, a notebook. The Cardinal might call at almost any hour to ask how he could reach a priest in another city, or to track down a bishop in another country. I developed a kind of pride in flicking through a reference book while he was still asking his question, popping the answer back as though I'd somehow topped the quizmaster in a television show. I had a private telephone line at the office, open to the Cardinal and a handful of others.

Because of the time zone difference, Cardinal Cody sometimes phoned Rome in the early hours of Chicago mornings. It might be four o'clock and pitch dark in Chicago, but it was already mid-morning with lunchtime approaching in Rome. By the end of Chicago's normal working day it was bedtime for many in Rome. Cardinal Wright used to complain that Vatican City telephone operators rang him at home with calls from tipsy Americans, rounding out a night at the neighborhood tavern with a phone call to the Pope to resolve a theological argument that followed a few beers.

The operators knew only one American and passed the calls along to Cardinal Wright. There may have been a law of reciprocity at work, because when he was the Bishop of Pittsburgh he was known to telephone local residents well after midnight to discuss letters of complaint that they'd mailed to him.

During a luncheon honoring the 1983 winner of the Cardinal Cody Communications Scholarship, Cardinal Bernardin recalled that he once received a telephone call from the late-working Bishop of Pittsburgh. The phone rang at about 2:30 in the morning. "Joe," asked Bishop Wright, "were you asleep?" Bishop Bernardin acknowledged that he had been asleep at that hour and his caller replied, "I always save my best call for the last."

Cardinal Cody was fascinated by communication equipment, starting with the telephone. He had more than one telephone number, including a super-private number that rang an instrument in his bedroom. I was always uneasy about using it, but he never complained and always managed, between yawns and while clearing his sleep-drained throat, to insist that he'd been awake anyway, no matter what the hour. In his residence he installed a word processor and a telex. He used the telex to send messages to Rome.

He told me that I was welcome to use it. Once, after a lengthy interview with Jaime Cardinal Sin in the Philippines I wrote a story for *The Chicago Catholic* and filed it by telex to the Cardinal's residence, with a request that a messenger be called to relay it promptly to the newspaper office. Cardinal Sin had spoken plainly about his distrust of the government. Cardinal Cody read the telex and decided not to forward it to *The Chicago Catholic* because he thought that the story could cause trouble for the Archbishop of Manila.

Later I explained that Cardinal Sin wanted to have his words read in the United States because they were largely ignored by the secular press, controlled or influenced by the government, in the Philippines. I also chose that time to install a telex at *The Chicago Catholic*.

Cardinal Cody was delighted by each development in communications. He provided solid backing for a Catholic television system that put the Archdiocese of Chicago far ahead of the Church generally in learning how to apply contemporary communication methods, especially as a tool in Catholic schools.

But there was criticism of his decision to spend money on a television network during a time of rising social and institutional needs. He cheered the installation of technologically advanced equipment at *The Chicago Catholic*. He encouraged the use of equipment to transmit letters and documents by telephone, especially valuable in his Office of Communications, which was designed to serve the needs of the news media and internal communication as well.

All of this became a part of Cardinal Bernardin's inheritance. Except for some of the details—he decided not to use his home as though it were his principal office, as Cardinal Cody did—he began at the outset to make effective use of it. He also knows how to use the telephone efficiently. His national and international roles, superimposed upon his Chicagoland duties, require the efficient use of time.

Despite what some might perceive as an innate shyness, what others might see as personal modesty, Cardinal Bernardin has communicated well and naturally for as long as anyone can remember. His childhood friends recall this as one of his spontaneous qualities. During his years in the episcopacy, communicating has taken on some additional dimensions.

Among those who have figured in the shaping of those dimensions are Daniel Kane, who handled media communication for Archbishop Bernardin in Cincinnati, and Robert Beusse, who became secretary of communication for the National Conference of Catholic Bishops and the United States Catholic Conference early in the Bernardin years. Dan Kane told me to be alert, not to let my personal admiration for Cardinal Bernardin push me into canonizing him prematurely; the advice seemed reasonable and probably originated with Bernardin.

Bob Beusse was 39 and Bishop Bernardin was 41 when the two met for the first time. "I remember being surprised when he called and said he wanted to meet me and was coming to New York to do that," Bob Beusse recalled. "It seemed unusual to me. I had grown accustomed as a lay volunteer in many aspects of Church work to being expected to appear where the Church leadership was. I was taken aback when Bishop Bernardin said he was coming to New York to meet me." At that time Bishop Bernardin was general secretary of the episcopal conference in Washington.

"We talked a bit about the Church and communications," Bob Beusse told me. "He talked about the fact that the Church was lagging in this area and needed to update itself, much as it was doing in so many other aspects of its life. He was anxious that there be a professional person heading up all of the conference's communication apparatus. He wanted someone who was imaginative and who could be a loyal member of his team. We had a relationship from the start that was charactertized by a deep sense of trust.

"I remember trusting him from the first moment I shook hands with him. He was direct. He was not someone who hestiated to deal with difficult problems. He began by saying that it would not be an easy economic matter for a person to leave the broadcasting industry and work for the bishops. He brought that up and wanted to deal with it. His way of dealing with it was to tell me to write out the substance of an agreement between the conference and myself. That conversation led to what I believe was the very first contract or letter of agreement between the United States Catholic Conference and a lay employee. It was a concept that was to be followed for other key leaders in the years to come, and all of it developed directly from the initiative of Bishop Bernardin."

It was arranged that Bob Beusse would work in New York. "Naturally we had the telephone and used that frequently. But from the beginning we resolved on periodic meetings. Sometimes these meetings were on a Saturday morning when the desks were clear and the phones weren't ringing and we could spend some time together. I would fly down to Washington. My procedure, which he seemed to like, was to give him a brief outline of perhaps four to eight or ten subjects that might have to be covered at a meeting. By the time we met he'd had a chance to read the agenda and any small documents I might attach to it.

"I was struck by the fact that he grasped things quickly and had a very sharp understanding of communications and what it could do for the Church. He had a way of coming to grips with the difficult elements on an agenda and easily moving aside matters that might otherwise rob us of valuable time.

"I was surprised by how deeply he had penetrated individual staff problems and how he waited for my appraisal to see whether it matched his. He may have his own judgments and his own sense of what needs to be done, but he clearly waits for that judgment to be supported or at least endorsed by others who have expertise in the area being dealt with. I always felt that he respected my position as department director. He did not try to supplant my authority in any way, but rather to reinforce it. As we got to know each other better, a phrase of his that became common in our relationship was this: 'You take the necessary actions. I'll back you.' Those two sentences perhaps give a clear picture of the way the man functions."

Bob Beusse noticed something else that has been noticed by others who work with Cardinal Bernardin. That's his total commitment to the person with whom he's talking or working. It is an ability to shut out everything else, to give his full attention to one thing at a time. He does this even when there are countless matters encroaching on his time and pulling at his mental faculties. This is an uncommon characteristic. Many busy leaders are preoccupied and distracted even while they are addressing important issues.

Cardinal Bernardin gives his total attention to the persons and issues before him and simply does not allow himself to be distracted or to have his time wasted. He shows his impatience, sometimes, when issues that are clearly understood are repeated or restated or paraphrased. He remains a gentleman, but his exasperation is plain enough to those who are sensitive to such things. He also does not get drawn into the impossible.

Sometimes a bishop is called upon to do more than he possibly can, even to do something that's forbidden by the Church. At that point Cardinal Bernardin may ask: "What do they want me to do? What do they expect that I can do?" Those questions do not simply express frustration, but they express what Bob Beusse calls the Cardinal's "honest search for what might be called the nth degree, the extra something that might bring about some reconciliation or some resolution of a trying problem."

When he has faced intransigence, obstinacy, obvious attempts to undermine his work and policies, his human side has been conspicuous. He suffers personally when he has to discipline a priest or an employee. He does everything that he can, and far more than most would do, to try to avoid unnecessary difficulty for others. Before discharging an employee he has actually put himself in touch with members of the family who might be affected, trying to reach out with loving support. His understanding of human relations is extensive.

In his famous address to priests working with Chicagoland Hispanics, Cardinal Bernardin spoke of his need for support, for approval, for gestures of affection and acceptance. He tries to provide that kind of support for those who work closely with him and depend in practical, human ways upon his approval and support.

Beyond all that, few bishops in the world understand the structure of the Catholic Church quite as well as Cardinal Bernardin does. He began building that understanding as a young bishop at the National Conference of Catholic Bishops. He respected the role of those who reported to him. He also knew how to apply the support, authority and resourcefulness of those to whom he reported on the Executive Committee and Administrative Board and within the full body of bishops. He worked with the Apostolic Delegate and served on committees in Rome. He learned how Vatican structures could be helpful in given situations. Cardinal Bernardin knows how to work within structures, including political structures. He knows how to get them to deliver results.

One result of this, whether at an episcopal conference or in the Church of Chicago, is excellence in administration. Nobody has ever observed him with his back to the wall, because he prepares himself—does his homework—and then he prepares others. Just when it seems that all possible resources have been utilized in meeting a major need, Cardinal Bernardin finds yet another way to approach the problem. That's not a random kind of thing. He does it over and over.

Sometimes his actions are so spontaneous and direct that

observers don't even realize that a problem has been overcome, that embarrassment has been avoided or that the
action springs out of the man's character and experience.
His travel party in Poland, when he was president of the
National Conference of Catholic Bishops, included
one layman. He was John T. Muthig, then chief of the
Rome Bureau of the National Catholic News Service.

As the group filed in for dinner in the residence of a
Polish bishop, John Muthig realized that no place had
been set for him. Just as he was trying to disappear into the
drapes, as he recalls it, Bishop Bernardin leaped to his feet,
invited the journalist to take his place at the table and
caused an extra place to be found in a hurry. Years later
that reporter became Father John Muthig, serving in the
Diocese of Trenton.

Bishop Bernardin was not distressed by his own embarrassment, either. After one of his rare short vacations
when he was general secretary he returned from Bermuda
laughing at himself, telling the story of riding a motorbike
that took off and went out of control, tossing the bishop
over a hedgerow and into someone's well-tended front
yard. He laughed hard about that and showed his ability to
laugh at himself.

Essentially, Cardinal Bernardin is one who communicates well with God through prayer, with others one-
on-one or collectively, even with himself without taking
himself too seriously.

That helps to explain why he is so popular with
reporters; he makes it easier for them to communicate his
positions to their readers, viewers and listeners. He reads
widely, listens well, turns to specialists for specialized
information, sifts it, makes his decisions and then
communicates them.

Chapter Fourteen

FEW Chicagoans realized that the man they had greeted with such enthusiasm a few months earlier, who had lived up to their happiest expectations and beyond, was a controversial figure. That position came to him uninvited after he was given the chairmanship of the ad hoc committee charged with drafting the famous pastoral letter on war and peace.

Father Roberto Tucci, the brilliant Jesuit who heads Vatican Radio, told Robert Beusse at the time of the Consistory that some critics attached political significance to the appointment of Archbishop Bernardin to Chicago. They felt that a political penalty would go with it. They thought that the Pope would be making a political statement concerning the East-West situation if he were to appoint the Cincinnati ordinary to Chicago.

However, Father Tucci observed, the criticism seemed to fade away after the appointment was made and especially after Pope John Paul II made Archbishop Bernardin the only American Cardinal appointed during the Consistory.

Simplistic descriptions had been attached to him. He was called the "anti-nuclear" bishop by reporters writing quickly and accustomed to using catch phrases. Reaction to the second draft of the collective pastoral letter was not uniformly approving, especially in the White House and in parts of Europe. How that reaction was met and how it began reshaping itself will be shown later. It was true, though, that Cardinal Bernardin was not always understood even by the generally friendly media, and it was not always easy to present his thoughtfully balanced ideas in a

131

few words at press time. His absolute fidelity to the Pope
has been a part of his thought from his earliest days
as a churchman. His ecumenical positions have never
weakened his assurance that the Roman Catholic Church
is unique and that its teachings are authentic, drawing
upon the life and example of Christ Jesus.

As an American he has no trouble understanding the
reasons why the state should not interfere with the Church.
During the national Bicentennial year he addressed this
issue in a homily at Cincinnati's Cathedral of St. Peter in
Chains. "A particular danger we face now is that of dis-
torting the proper relationship between church and state,"
he said.

"The wise dictum of the First Amendment of our
Constitution that the government must establish no state
religion and must not interfere in the internal affairs of
churches is frequently and incorrectly used today as a man-
date that religious or moral values have no place in
American public life. Surely this is the thrust of some of
the decisions of the Supreme Court in recent years."

He criticized what might be called the civil religion of
secularism and said: "A study of our history from the very
beginning clearly shows that religion has been a crucial factor in our growth and development. It is evident to all that
our destiny as a nation has been shaped to a significant
extent by our Judaeo-Christian heritage."

He tackled the question of religion and politics head on
in a *Chicago Catholic* column on December 3, 1982. I
thought it was so important that I began it on the front
page. It attracted attention all over the country. In that
column Archbishop Bernardin said that he'd received
some letters about the proposed pastoral on war and peace

that admonished the bishops to "stay out of politics."

He wrote: "Whether it be abortion or human rights in Central America, racial justice or nuclear weapons policy, whenever bishops or church-related groups take a stand on a public issue a predictable chorus goes up, 'Stay out of politics!' To some extent it's a question of whose ox is being gored. Critics of the Catholic bishops' activism on abortion rarely object to their efforts against racism."

He explained: "As a matter of fidelity to the Gospel, the Church sometimes—indeed, often—advocates positions which challenge secular values and widely-held prejudices. Abortion is a good example. From the very beginning of the Christian era the deliberate destruction of unborn human life has been firmly, unequivocally condemned as a grievous wrong."

He went on to say: "Hence, the firm commitment, on the part of the Catholic Church and also many other churches and religious bodies, to changing the law on abortion. For it was the Supreme Court's radical and arbitrary change in the law through its 1973 decisions which led directly to the present state of affairs. But this stance directly challenges the views and values of people who have made a commitment to abortion as a convenient solution to social problems, as a private 'right' or whatever. So the battle is joined. And the pro-abortionists, feeling angry and threatened, resort by instinct to the argument that religion should keep out of politics."

It is characteristic of Cardinal Bernardin that although he believes religious groups have as much right to express their views as any other groups, they should not claim that theirs are the only views that can be held by persons of good will.

The argument that the Church has no right to talk about gun control, racial discrimination, capital punishment, abortion, indiscriminate warfare and other moral questions reflects, the Cardinal has said, a schizophrenic attitude on the part of some Americans, including some Catholic Americans. And on the other hand the hierarchy has been criticized for being slow to speak out on public policy, as in the case of the Vietnam war.

He applied his substantial influence at the time of the 1983 election for a mayor of Chicago, calling upon everyone in the community to rise above racism. He acknowledged that he should not become a spokesperson for partisan politics. He could observe that tensions were growing between supporters of Harold Washington, a black and a Protestant, and Bernard Epton, a white and a Jew.

"On the basis of what I have read and heard," he wrote in *The Chicago Catholic* on March 18, 1983 "there seems to be little doubt that racism is a factor in the current mayoral campaign." He thought there was little to be said for choosing a candidate on the basis of race: "My basic plea to the white and black communities is that racism not be permitted to become a factor in the campaign—racism that would cause one to vote for or against a candidate solely because of color."

After he saw that one of the candidates included a picture of him in television commercials he asked that his picture be withdrawn. He took a non-partisan position but one that was morally clear, and doubtless influential, in reducing the level of racial distrust.

I do not know how he voted in that election. It is not surprising that a South Carolina native considered himself a Democrat early in life, but he has told friends that he votes according to his preference for candidates and not out of party attachment. It is not surprising, either, that a contemporary South Carolina native should work hard to overcome racial prejudice wherever it might appear. Each of the two Chicago candidates came from minority groups that have received friendly and sympathetic attention from Cardinal Bernardin for many years.

His predecessor in Chicago faced considerable resentment when he arrived in town. As the Archbishop of New Orleans during a period when U.S. racial policies were being energetically updated at every level he was outspoken in support of desegregation. This did not please everyone in Chicago when his appointment was announced.

Cardinal Cody told me, just a few months after he became the Archbishop of Chicago, that there had been threats on his life. He said that he made it a practice to travel in various cars and to change his routes because he had been advised to do so to guard against possible assault. By the time Chicago's 1983 election came there had been an enormous improvement in race relations, but Cardinal Bernardin found it necessary to reaffirm Catholic teaching on the subject.

The development of an orderly society based upon law and reflecting a high moral code is one of the goals of Christians generally, and of many others. Cardinal Bernardin spoke of this in an address to the Chicago Bar Association in April of 1983. He observed that Americans, among others, have a long tradition of respect, even reverence, for the law. "And though it may only rarely be adverted to consciously," he told the lawyers, "the root of that respect and reverence goes back to the Jewish people's belief that the Law, the Torah, was of God."

He then said that all who share the Judaeo-Christian tradition are heirs to that belief, whether they know it or not. He rejected the blind acceptance of every law, regardless of whether it is good or bad. He told the legal specialists that they "help preserve respect for all law by critiquing and criticizing those bad laws which can only serve to generate contempt for law itself."

Every modern American who hails gains for members of minority races knows, or ought to know, that human slavery was once the law of the land. The United States Supreme Court upheld slavery. After slavery was extinguished in consequence of a long, bloody war that same Supreme Court of the United States ruled that "separate but equal" treatment of blacks was justified, that blacks could be given separate schools and ordered to sit in the back of the bus.

Many Americans refused to accept the judgment of the Supreme Court as representing either good law or sound morality, just as many Americans today are horrified by the Supreme Court's decision that unborn infants have no ordinary human rights and may be disposed of at the whim of what the court seems to see as owners rather than parents.

Cardinal Bernardin has spoken of other examples of the unfair application of laws: "For example, the more affluent can get out on bail while the poor must remain in jail for months just awaiting arraignment; legal assistance available to those who can afford a lawyer is usually superior to that available to those who cannot afford their own attorney. These are not just legal problems; they also raise serious moral questions."

During a Mass for Catholic lawyers and jurists Cardinal

Bernardin said that all practitioners of the law are servants of justice, servants of truth and servants of love. As servants of justice they work against all forms of discrimination, inequality and inequity. As servants of truth they struggle against the temptation to compromise their integrity.

As servants of love they try to resist the idea of overzealous advocacy, a concern that was addressed in April of 1983 by Derek C. Bok, the president of Harvard University. President Bok, a lawyer, said in his annual report to the Board of Overseers of Harvard College that the whole legal system is too costly and complicated. He said that this results in a spurious form of justice that favors the privileged and puts too much emphasis on confrontation.

Cardinal Bernardin anticipated President Bok's position in his homily in 1982 and in his talk to the Chicago Bar Association. In that talk he referred to some advice that Abraham Lincoln had for lawyers: "Discourage litigation. Persuade your neighbors to compromise whenever you can, point out to them how the nominal winner is often a real loser—in fees, expenses and waste of time." Cardinal Bernardin asked the members of the legal profession to be peacemakers.

Much of what gets presented as church-state confrontation has its beginnings in the early prejudices of a country that had few Roman Catholics in its first days. Public education, which developed out of church-sponsored education, was largely Protestant in its outlook.

As time passed public education moved gradually from a Protestant orientation to a frankly secularist point of view, with religion largely ignored as a significant part of life. All sorts of subjects were recognized as important. They included history, language, driver education, football, government, natural sciences, mathematics and literature, but they did not include religion.

Public schools began to provide professional counselors, who worked with individual youngsters to help solve their personal problems and direct them into a balanced future. No religious counseling was available under the system that grew in school districts throughout the country. It might be that more Americans went to religious services than to sports events on weekends, but sports could be taught in the schools and religion was officially seen as having nothing to do with education.

Each group of citizens, religious and non-religious, was taxed equally but all of the money was spent on education that met exclusively non-religious standards. This is plainly undemocratic, but it is hard to beat the system. As school taxation rises, citizens have less of their own money left to spend on education of their own choice.

Cardinal Bernardin has said that the debate over tuition tax credits does not concern money alone, but the principle of fairness. He asked this question in a newspaper column: "Do parents who pay as much as anyone else—through their tax dollars—to support public education have a right to modest assistance from government for some (but by no means all) of the added burden they bear in exercising their option to choose church-related and private schooling for their children? For me, the answer is clearly yes."

Cardinal Bernardin speaks out whenever moral issues are debated on the political scene. He's been doing that for a long time. He was installed as the Archbishop of Cincinnati on December 19, 1972. He decided that during his first

Christmas Midnight Mass in the Cincinnati cathedral he would speak out against the bombing in Vietnam.

Immediately after that Christmas it was announced that Archbishop Bernardin was one of three church leaders invited by President Nixon to speak at an ecumenical service in the White House. That was the time of the second Nixon inauguration, when there was growing distress about Vietnam and when there were whispers of Watergate.

There were some in Cincinnati who thought that Archbishop Bernardin ought to use the White House event as an occasion to criticize Administration policies in a clear and powerful way. Dan Kane, who was the Archbishop's media aide, recalls that Archbishop Bernardin rejected such suggestions, explaining that he would be the guest of the President for an ecumenical service of prayer. It would not be an appropriate time or place for such remarks. He decided instead to say something about his hope that national leaders would be responsive to the needs of the poor and that justice would prevail in social legislation.

He worked hard on that White House talk. He crafted it carefully and gave it a positive tone. At the prayer service Billy Graham spoke out for teaching the Ten Commandments in public schools. His talk received some media attention, but it was Archbishop Bernardin's remarks which drew extensive coverage.

Cardinal Bernardin's strong conviction that individual rights are precious has caused him to take positions that are not necessarily popular with everyone. He takes a close look at the issues before he speaks, and that sometimes means that he adds heavily to his normal burden of reading and research. His friends know that he has within him an enormous capacity for hard work and that he will respond to all of the needs of any organization or committee which he heads. Much of his success in carrying out all of that work comes from his capacity for setting priorities.

Anyone who has worked closely with him has seen how he is able to concentrate strongly in one or two or three areas until they are moving to his satisfaction, then quickly move on to a whole variety of new tasks that he may have set aside temporarily while directing his tremendous energy to priority projects and programs. He plunges into the sundry other tasks with the same vigor that he applies to the major tasks. If he seems to be concentrating in one area, give him a little time and you'll see him working on a broad spectrum of other interests with identical energy.

Setting priorities and holding to them is one of the personal qualities that enables him to accomplish so much. He has all of these qualities about him when he addresses the complex issues in which the interests of church and state overlap. His determination to support a free and fair state is as powerful as his assertion of the rights and obligations of a free and fair church.

Chapter Fifteen

JOHN Henry Cardinal Newman said that the real love of humankind depends upon practice. It does not come from talking about love, even from being well-disposed toward everybody and ready to help. Real love of humankind "must begin by exercising itself on our friends around us, for otherwise it will have no existence," Cardinal Newman said.

"By trying to love our relations and friends, by submitting to their wishes, though contrary to our own, by bearing with their infirmities, by overcoming their occasional waywardness by kindness, by dwelling on their excellencies, and trying to copy them, thus it is that we form in our hearts that root of charity, which, though small at first, may, like the mustard seed, at last even overshadow the earth."

If you go back to South Carolina to talk with former school chums, or if you go to Northern Italy to visit the Bernardin family, if you track down the priests and laity who shared much of his life in Washington, if you get into conversations in Cincinnati or Chicago, you will find that Joseph Bernardin has always been friendly and that he keeps his friends.

He's not one to suffer fools gladly. His face and eyes sometimes show disbelief and with it a sort of injured feeling. He tries to be honest with others and expects honesty in return. The higher the office a person holds, the more difficult it may be to get altogether honest and unshaded information from others. There may be an anxiety to please or a more compelling anxiety to avoid displeasing, to conceal at least part of the truth and some of the facts.

He enjoys good company. Naturally enough, he's likely to be in priestly company during most of his relaxed moments at home or taking walks with friends. Not long before he moved to Chicago I returned from dinner in Cincinnati with Judy Ball, editor of *The Catholic Telegraph*. I was walking toward my hotel in the early evening when from across the street I was hailed by two men, both casually dressed and vaguely disturbing to a lone pedestrian after sunset on a downtown sidewalk. Eventually my caution eased and I decided to acknowledge the waves from the strangers in the shadows.

When I looked closely I saw the Archbishop of Cincinnati and his administrative assistant, Father Thomas C. Nolker. They were out for their regular walk, unrecognized by the few who were strolling or driving by. Cardinal Bernardin enjoys a walk with a friend and the relaxed conversation that goes with it.

His home is in one of Chicago's choice areas for a pleasant walk. It faces the southern end of Lincoln Park, which trails Lake Michigan for miles northward. The Lincoln Park Zoo is about ten minutes on foot from the residence, which is in an area of expensive homes and condominiums.

When I spoke to Cardinal Cody about finding a place to live in Chicago he told me that his area was fine, but went on to explain that I would find it too expensive. I replied that he could easily correct that situation, but he preferred to chuckle at my wisecrack. During his years in the residence at 1555 North State Parkway some of the neighbors denied that he lived there. They saw so little of him in the neighborhood, saw so few lights burning at night, that they thought he had an apartment someplace else and used the mammoth home simply as a place to work. I called on him there a couple of hundred times.

He often answered the door himself and when I visited him early I often found him alone. One Monday morning he told me that he'd been ill over the weekend and had eaten nothing because he didn't feel up to preparing anything. Cardinal Bernardin couldn't find himself in that lonely condition, because even the neighbors know that the house is occupied, that lights burn from many windows and that it is hospitable to many guests.

One of Cardinal Bernardin's best known characteristics is his interest in those who are around him, whether they are around him a lot at home or in the office or whether they are standing in a reception line. He's noted for giving total attention to one person at a time. In one Chicago parish, just after she'd met the Cardinal following Mass, a woman remarked about his concentration on what she was saying and on his eyes connecting firmly with her own. "His look was so penetrating," she said to a friend, "that I was glad I'd been to Confession."

Communicating with one person at a time is obviously important to Cardinal Bernardin, who also is skilled in communicating with large groups, including the whole country if he thinks that's necessary. He polished some of his native skills when he was general secretary of the National Conference of Catholic Bishops and the United States Catholic Conference. During that time the U.S.C.C. Department of Communications developed a training program for bishops that included exercises in television techniques. They were held in such places as Howard University in Washington, Notre Dame University in

Indiana and Loyola University in New Orleans.

It wasn't easy to get the general secretary away from his work for a week, so a special arrangement was made with the American Broadcasting Company television studios in Washington. By making use of studio downtime, an hour here and ninety minutes there, the Communications Department managed to provide training sessions for Bishop Bernardin with the help of network personnel.

Anyone who has ever heard Cardinal Bernardin answer a journalist's question or explain an elaborately complex situation without notes is aware of an occasional hesitation in his voice as he forms his thoughts into words. That hesitation is part of his search for precision in language. He has an unusual ability to parse his own sentences as he speaks and he seldom chooses an imprecise word. If you'll read the transcript of a press interview you will find that it is virtually without error and needs little editing. That's in stark contrast to many public figures who speak off the cuff and then wish they hadn't.

Few laymen have observed the Bernardin manner more closely than Daniel Kane. He told me that Cardinal Bernardin's relations with the media had always been extremely healthy. It has never been his style to avoid the media, even when contacts may be strenuous. One reason for this is that he generally is well prepared on the subject at hand. He doesn't have to search for answers; he searches in his mind only for the most exact way to express the answers.

Peter Foote, head of the communications office for the Archdiocese of Chicago, describes Cardinal Bernardin as a man who effectively handles his own media relations and depends upon the communications staff to provide necessary support to reporters and photographers, to see that arrangements are made for television crews and that copies of talks are reproduced for the press.

There is such a demand upon his time, there are so many requests for interviews from all over the world, that a communications director does not have to search for outlets. Much of his work calls for tact and sensitivity when the Cardinal's schedule remains overloaded for weeks at a time.

There's nothing really different in the way Cardinal Bernardin talks with a reporter and the way he talks with a parishioner in a stretched-out receiving line. He gives his full attention and his best answers. Despite what sometimes appears to be a native shyness, not unheard of in public figures, he plainly enjoys talking with people. That joy is not diminished by the need to hide anything. The feeling is almost universally reciprocated, and Cardinal Bernardin is enormously satisfying to most journalists.

Roy Larson, an Episcopalian and former Methodist clergyman who gained national recognition as the religion editor of the Chicago *Sun-Times*, has written perceptively of the Bernardin personality and accomplishments. Roy Larson was sharply critical of Cardinal Cody; there were some who thought that his criticisms might lead to a Pulitzer Prize. Cardinal Cody declined to talk with him, but Roy Larson found the Cody successor to be entirely open and highly respected by those who knew him at first hand, such as Benjamin L. Kaufman, religion editor of the *Cincinnati Enquirer.*

Cardinal Bernardin's respect for Bruce Buursma, religion specialist for the *Chicago Tribune*, has been well founded. Long before he moved to Chicago, Cardinal Bernardin had sound relationships with admired professionals such as George W. Cornell of the Associated Press, Kenneth Briggs of *The New York Times*, Laura Petrie of the *Cincinnati Post*, Russell Chandler of the *Los Angeles Times*, Marjorie Hyer of the *Washington Post*, and many others from all over the country. He's on terms of shared respect with radio and television journalists and his face is familiar to network viewers.

James L. Kilcoyne, who began working in 1950 as photographer for *The New World*, which was to become *The Chicago Catholic*, had an uncompromising affection and respect for Cardinal Cody and immediately developed the same feeling for Cardinal Bernardin. Probably no newsperson was with Cardinal Bernardin as often as Jim Kilcoyne during the Cardinal's first months in Chicago.

Cardinal Bernardin's relationship with writers for the *New York Times*, *Time*, *Newsweek*, the *Wall Street Journal* and other nationally-circulated publications was based upon trust as far back as his years in Washington. Journalists for the Catholic press, especially observant of his ways as a bishop, valued his considerate treatment of the religious media from the start of his career. He favored open meetings of the bishops and was not inclined to patronize the Catholic press, recognizing that it reaches some twenty million subscribers in a nation of some fifty million Catholics, men, women and children. He was general secretary for the bishops when in 1971 Pope Paul VI approved in its entirety the Pastoral Instruction for the Application of the Decree of the Second Ecumenical Council on the Means of Social Communication. That document is largely about freedom of information, although its title plainly was not the work of a headline writer for either the press or television. The editor of a widely circulated Catholic magazine told me about a letter that he'd received from a bishop who complained that an article published in the magazine had spoken of different points of view about the ordination of women. That's not a proper subject for discussion in or out of print, the bishop suggested, because the matter has been settled and the subject closed. The editor grinned, without much humor, and shrugged his shoulders. He wondered how the Church's teaching on the whole subject of ordination and vocations to Church service can be presented convincingly if nobody is allowed to talk about it.

Cardinal Bernardin is publicly committed to the ordination of men and only men to the priesthood, but his comprehension of the Pastoral Instruction on Social Communication perhaps sustains a natural American interest in free discussion—even if what's said is wrong. It puts his thinking and that of most U.S. journalists on the same track. Men are, after all, ordained year after year and women are not. That's bound to raise questions among the inquisitive and the questions deserve the kind of answer Cardinal Bernardin is not hesitant to provide.

Public opinion, the Pastoral Instruction observes, changes often. The document says: "The same idea sometimes gains and sometimes loses hold of the public. Because of this, it is prudent to maintain a certain detachment towards the opinions currently in vogue. There may well be good reasons that require one to oppose them. However, views openly and commonly expressed which reflect the aspirations of people should always be carefully considered. This is especially binding on those in authority, whether civil or religious.''

That puts quite a burden on bishops, but Cardinal Bernardin seems to recognize the opportunity for teaching and persuading that goes with it. That's why he talks as spontaneously and precisely to a high school student with a notebook in hand as he does to a wire service correspondent with a notebook in hand.

Not every bishop works at communicating the way Cardinal Bernardin does. Sharing information freely with the media is an idea that came relatively recently to the Catholic Church. Not even the most adroit politican, no matter how heavily shielded from the effects of criticism, enjoys answering pointed questions from an aggressive press.

It was remarkable back in the 1950s for John J. Wright, the first Bishop of Worcester, Massachusetts, to hold frequent press conferences and to make himself available to reporters at almost any time. Bishop Wright felt that if reporters could not obtain accurate information readily they could not be blamed for going to press with only part of the truth. His plan worked well at the time. Now virtually every diocese has a professional media relations official who is available to reporters and has ready access to the bishop. All of that is taken for granted now, but it developed almost entirely during the second part of the twentieth century. After he became the Bishop of Pittsburgh and then when he became the Cardinal Prefect of the Sacred Congregation for the Clergy in Rome, Cardinal Wright remained open to the media. Visiting reporters often sat at his dinner table just a short walk from St. Peter's Square. Cardinal Bernardin would see nothing peculiar about that.

One of my last evenings with Cardinal Wright in Rome came at the time of the Conclave which was to elect Pope John Paul II. I had been one of the lucky journalists who drew lots for a visit to the Sistine Chapel, where the papal electors were to assemble, and to the quarters in which they were to eat and sleep. My tour of the venerable premises ended shortly before I joined an ailing Cardinal Wright for dinner. He was as inquisitive as ever, filled then with questions about the quarters he was to occupy for the election. The Cardinal walked with difficulty and was to be accompanied to the Conclave by his long-time secretary, Father Donald Wuerl, later rector of Pittsburgh's St. Paul Seminary.

Although Cardinal Wright was in the late stages of an illness that would shortly take his life, he was as up to date as a journalist on the news of the world. He spoke of developments behind the Iron Curtain, insisting that the Vatican had better sources of accurate information than most major governments had. He had an intense interest in the world and its people, and that quality is apparent in Cardinal Bernardin.

I'd spent most of my life in the secular press before becoming editor of *The Catholic Review* in Baltimore during the time of the Second Vatican Council. The publisher asked me about a story that appeared in the edition he'd just read. It is not common to describe publishers as saintly, because publishers often have things on their mind that do not encourage saintlike behavior.

Lawrence Cardinal Shehan, then the Archbishop of Baltimore, was the saintly publisher who called my attention to a news report that, he said, he didn't like. That's good, I said, because if a publisher can read all the way through a newspaper without spotting a single news story that he disagrees with there's something wrong with his editor. An editor ought to make certain that various points of view are represented in news stories, granting that a single viewpoint may appear in editorials.

Cardinal Shehan agreed. He kept his expectations high. He thought that truth is valuable and during his years as archbishop he advocated nothing less. Ironically, it was a reorganization plan for the United States Catholic Conference, with Bishop Bernardin its general secretary, that led to a later observation by Cardinal Shehan. I wrote in an editorial that the reorganization could create the impression that the professional independence of the National Catholic News Service had not been taken into account as fully as it might have been.

I was cautious about including the news agency within the department that also handled public relations and media relations and said so. Cardinal Shehan told me that he did not agree with all that I had written. "But," he added, "you're the editor and you should write what you think." In fact it probably was the only time that we disagreed on anything of any importance. Cardinal Shehan did not need to add as a postscript a reminder that an editor should think before writing, then accept the responsibility for what has been written.

Cardinal Cody had a strong commitment to Catholic communications. He thought that Catholic newspapers were essential to Catholic life, and that thought was in accord with the Pastoral Instruction on Social Communications. Deacon Sydney J. Mench, a newspaper consultant and retired circulation manager of the *Chicago Sun-Times*, observed in homilies delivered after Cardinal Bernardin became the Archbishop of Chicago that the Pastoral Instruction plainly calls for support of the Catholic press by all Catholics.

Cardinal Cody supported Catholic press, television and radio activities. He did not accept, as Cardinal Shehan did, the idea that he should not be able to read his newspaper all the way through without finding reports of actions he didn't find agreeable. He made no secret of that view. He sometimes thought of his newspaper, to the dismay of many, as a house organ rather than an authentic newspaper, official but nevertheless both catholic and Catholic.

Cardinal Bernardin arrived in Chicago with a number of personal advantages, including his long and healthy relationship with the media. He already valued journalism and journalists, who knew that he would work with them to the outer limits of honesty and integrity. He was a man of the times, entirely comfortable with people and at ease with the media. If there hadn't already been a Pastoral Instruction on Social Communications he could have written one.

Chapter Sixteen

PERHAPS no other nation in modern times developed the spiritual and psychological self-examination that blanketed the United States after the Vietnam war. It was not, for the United States, a war of conquest. But gradually the country came to feel that it was engaged almost accidentally in the wrong war in the wrong place for the wrong reasons. Even returning veterans felt a sort of national cold shoulder, an attempt to sweep the whole episode away.

Anxieties growing out of the war years intruded into almost every area of foreign policy, anxieties that were stimulated by the threat of nuclear destruction. Headlines told of new wars and the rekindling of old wars in Afghanistan, Iran, Iraq, Lebanon, Central America. The domestic struggle for money to pay for social needs collided with demands for new and costly approaches to defense.

There were quarrels about the definition of defense, especially in relation to the creation of weapons that could be applied to offense strategies.

When the Catholic bishops of the United States met in the fall of 1980 they shared the country's concerns. There was no way to shrug them off, and the temptation to do so was easily overcome. Many of the bishops were sensitive to the Vietnam issue. Some felt that the hierarchy had been slow to insist on the withdrawal of American forces from the jungles of Southeast Asia. They were ready to take a somber look at the threat of war and to offer leadership for peace.

Archbishop John R. Roach of St. Paul and Minneapolis

was president of the National Conference of Catholic Bishops. He looked to a former president, then Archbishop of Cincinnati, to chair an ad hoc committee that would examine the war and peace question from every reasonable direction. That examination was to take nearly two years and to explore theological, scriptural, military, pastoral and diplomatic concerns.

Archbishop Bernardin was named chairman in January 1981 and by spring four members were named to serve with him. They were Bishops Daniel P. Reilly of Norwich, Conn.; George A. Fulcher, then auxiliary in Columbus, Ohio, and later the Bishop of Lafayette, Ind.; Thomas J. Gumbleton, auxiliary of Detroit; and John J. O'Connor, then auxiliary to the military vicar for the armed forces. After the final draft of the pastoral was approved he was named Bishop of Scranton.

In July 1981 the formal work began. During the next year there would be fourteen meetings; by November 1981 Archbishop Bernardin was able to report to the annual meeting of the bishops that progress had been made. At that time he gave his fellow bishops an overview of the state of Catholic teaching on nuclear weapons and went on to strike a prophetic tone. He asked whether the time had come for a "new judgment" on moral issues of nuclear war and specifically of nuclear deterrence.

The committee was at work, hearing witnesses and approaching the first draft of a collective pastoral letter that would eventually reach out to the whole world. Archbishop Bernardin decided on a course of action which he believed would help assure freedom of discussion for committee members and staff consultants.

Until the first draft was completed and sent to all of the

bishops the following June he would give no interviews about the document and would not react to news stories about the work in progress. He would not be drawn into public discussion of the views of any members of the committee, although the committee members were free to speak and write as they pleased. Above all, he would not become an advocate to the public.

As the months passed this course of action became difficult to sustain. His principal media assistant in Cincinnati, Daniel Kane, spent a fair amount of time explaining his archbishop's decision. Some journalists understood the decision and some were skeptical, but Archbishop Bernardin held fast. Dan Kane learned then that the Archbishop of Cincinnati was held in high personal regard by journalists who accepted, one after another, rejection of their requests for interviews.

In the face of public confusion about the process which the drafting committee followed, Archbishop Bernardin decided that it was time to give some informal and off-the-record background briefings limited strictly to the process. "I was in the office with him during some of these telephone conversations," Dan Kane recalled, "and can attest to how helpful the briefings were, how precise and clear were his explanations of the process, how well he succeeded in all of this without giving any indication of the content of committee discussions."

The committee's direction became clear to the country's bishops in June 1982, when a different kind of bishops' meeting was held in Collegeville, Minn. It was a special gathering for prayer and reflection, with the media on the outside. The bishops had received the first draft in time to talk about it in Collegeville, and the media had more than a hint of the subject matter.

The document was marked "confidential," but copies were soon in circulation among reporters. Cardinal Bernardin observed the "confidential" nature of the document and guarded against leaks to the press in his own territory. *The Chicago Catholic* staff asked for no special favors, assuming that it wouldn't get them anyway, and put feelers out in Washington, Rome, New York—almost anywhere outside of Chicago. There were headlines everywhere, and in September Archbishop Bernardin said that response had been overwhelming.

Interest was so high, he said, that the bishops ought to have time to discuss it more thoroughly before voting on it. He proposed to submit a second draft to the National Conference of Catholic Bishops at its scheduled meeting November 15-18, 1982, but to defer a vote. In October that draft was released, and it was the major subject for discussion during the November meeting at the Capitol Hilton in Washington. In fact, it took up about half of the entire meeting.

While the sessions were in progress the White House decided to intervene, but it did so in a curious way. When Archbishop Bernardin picked up a copy of *The New York Times* at the Capitol Hilton newsstand he read for the first time the text of a letter addressed to him by the White House. He didn't receive the letter until after he'd read about it in the newspaper.

It was a lengthy letter about the second draft of the pastoral letter. What did Archbishop Bernardin think about reading the letter from William P. Clark, President Reagan's national security adviser, in a newspaper before he and others attending the annual meeting of the bishops received copies? "That unusual point is not important to us," he told me at the time. "We'd rather deal with ideas and not be concerned about the way in which they are communicated.'' He said he thought that the advance release of the letter to a newspaper was of little importance.

It may have caused more irritation among reporters who were scooped by the omnipresent *Times* than it did among the members of the hierarchy. ''We do not intend to give a substantive response,'' Archbishop Bernardin said as I wrote rapidly in my notebook during a brief conversation in the hotel. He pointed out that the committee had invited the Administration to respond at the same time that copies of the second draft were sent to all who testified, including representatives of the Administration and about a hundred others.

The Clark letter argued that the Reagan Administration was guided by moral principles in developing its policies on nuclear weapons. The letter said: ''The strategy of deterrence on which our policies are based is not an end in itself but a means to prevent war and preserve the values we cherish.'' It went on to say that the ''compelling'' moral considerations guiding the Administration were not shared by the Soviet Union. When I asked Archbishop Bernardin about that at the time, he said: ''Does that mean we should not consider the moral issue? We must be able to address the issue from a moral perspective.''

The second draft which was stimulating so much comment in the White House and elsewhere was 25,000 words long. There were an additional 2,700 words of footnotes. The bishops had studied the document before going to Washington, where they carried out round table discussions in small groups. After the round table discussions, 195 bishops were in agreement with the basic thrust of the document. Only twelve were in basic disagreement and 71 had major reservations. The document was praised by Archbishop Raymond G. Hunthausen of Seattle while Archbishop Philip M. Hannan of New Orleans said it ought to be scrapped.

Over and over, from the platform and in news conferences that were jammed with reporters and cameras, Archbishop Bernardin made it plain that the bishops were asking the American people to think about vital issues but were not trying to tell them what they must think. The moral imperative, he said patiently each time the question was asked, was to avoid all wars and especially to avoid nuclear wars. He made it plain that the bishops could not give a moral analysis of every conceivable use of weapons or change in military strategy. "People of good will who accept principles can differ on application," he said.

During one of the brightly-lit news conferences Archbishop Bernardin responded to a claim made by a syndicated columnist that he had been summoned to Rome by a Pope who reportedly was unhappy with the draft. Absolutely untrue, the Archbishop said, recalling that he had attended a long-scheduled meeting of the Council of the World Synod of Bishops. During an audience that included other bishops, he explained, he spoke one sentence to Pope John Paul II: "Holy Father, everything is going well in Chicago!" The Washington meeting ended with an agreement that there would be an extraordinary national meeting in Chicago's Palmer House May 2-3, 1983 to consider a third draft.

Before that meeting came about another conversation, of a different nature, was held in Vatican City. The Bernardin Committee, as it came to be known, sent copies of the first and second drafts to episcopal conferences in other countries to keep them informed and to give them an opportunity to comment if they wished. In January 1983 the Holy See convened an informal two-day meeting that brought U.S., European and Vatican representatives together to talk about the pastoral. Archbishops Roach and Bernardin were there.

It was a closed meeting and those who took part agreed not to talk about it publicly. They agreed that a synthesis would be prepared by Father Jan Schotte, secretary of the Pontifical Justice and Peace Commission. This was included in a confidential report mailed to U.S. bishops March 21, 1983 and published in *Origins*, the weekly documentary publication of the National Catholic News Service in Washington.

According to *Origins*, a January 25, 1983 memorandum from Archbishop Roach and Cardinal Bernardin to the U.S. hierarchy described the Vatican discussions as "primarily theological and ecclesiological, not political or strategic." In the course of an unrelated interview Cardinal Bernardin told me that the pastoral letter was an American document prepared by American bishops. It attempted to apply general principles of Catholic teaching to the American scene, to American realities. It is entirely in keeping with conciliar and papal teaching.

There were a few critics who thought that the whole pastoral letter was not quite American, at least in its claims for peace and justice. The second draft was denounced in some newspaper editorials because it seemed too idealistic in a tough world. Some conservative Catholics argued that it was unrealistic to expect cooperation for peace from the Soviet Union.

The ad hoc committee listened, read, sifted. It was at work on a major new draft, the third and, nearly everyone hoped, the final draft. Even while that work was in progress a group called Catholics for Responsible Action asked that the special meeting planned for Chicago be postponed, and that the bishops meanwhile adopt as their pastoral letter Pope John Paul II's message to the United Nations Second Special Session of the General Assembly on Disarmament in June 1982.

When the third draft appeared in April 1983 there was much to ponder. The pastoral, called "The Challenge of Peace: God's Promise and Our Response," had grown to 44,000 words. It was not simply longer. It was more precisely nuanced than the previous draft. It said that first use of nuclear weapons is an unjustifiable moral risk, that deterrence cannot be an end in itself but must lead to progressive disarmament.

It called for bilateral, verifiable agreements to curb the testing, production and deployment of new nuclear weapons systems—and from that call there came a flurry of comments. The second draft had called for a "halt" and the third draft for a "curb." The White House hailed the change, which was urged within the committee, according to the National Catholic News Service, by Bishop O'Connor. The new word was sharply assailed by liberals, some of whom charged that the bishops had caved in to Administration and European pressures.

In its spring 1983 issue the prestigious quarterly *Foreign Affairs* took a look at the pastoral letter. L. Bruce van Voorst, a *Time* correspondent, began by quoting Cardinal Bernardin: "Because the nuclear issue is not simply political, but also a profoundly moral and religious question, the Church must be a participant in the process of protecting the world and its people from the specter of nuclear destruction.''

The writer then observed: "On any single Sunday, almost as many Americans attend church services as go to all the major sporting events held in this country during an entire year. From its very origins, the United States has claimed a belief in a unique ethical foundation, a nation, as G. K. Chesterton said, 'with the soul of a church.' '' He commented that "many contemporary pronouncements by the clergy suggest a newly widespread determination among the churches to challenge public policy on nuclear issues.'' He observed that Prohibition came and went as a Protestant campaign and quoted the eminent Chicago Protestant church historian Martin Marty as calling "the ill-fated Kellogg-Briand Treaty 'virtually a Protestant document.' ''

The Foreign Affairs article described the draft pastoral letter as being "by far the most radical effort by any American church to define moral standards for the nuclear era.'' It said also that the nuclear issue has been debated "relatively longer and more intensely within the Protestant denominations,'' but "the historical Protestant treatment of the nuclear issues differs considerably from the current Catholic initiative,'' predictably "fragmented and dis-parate'' even though it began early.

The considerable attention given to the pastoral draft and to other religious activities directed toward world peace illustrates the broad reach of that effort and its intense interest to the readers of a distinguished magazine that specializes in foreign policy issues.

There were other articles in newspapers, magazines and

newsletters. There were countless letters to the editor. There were television interviews and radio commentaries. The whole world was watching when the U.S. bishops began a strenuous two-day meeting in Chicago on May 2, 1983.

By an overwhelming vote of 238 to 9 the bishops declared peace on the world, but only after they had considered some 500 proposed amendments. In a near-miracle of parliamentary procedure, the bishops completed their work within minutes of their scheduled adjournment.

Meanwhile they had accepted 174 amendments, generally following the recommendations of the ad hoc committee. There were standing ovations, with the bishops hailing the pastoral as a personal triumph for Cardinal Bernardin.

After the debate was over and the votes were counted, the document rejected nuclear war and called on everyone to work energetically for world peace. It returned to the demand for a "halt" in the "testing, production and deployment of new nuclear weapons systems." It rejected all forms of war except as a last resort. It questioned the morality of nuclear war in any form, including "limited" nuclear war. It said that it is "morally unjustifiable" to begin a nuclear war, calling for the rapid development of non-nuclear defense strategies. It presented a "strictly conditioned moral acceptance" of deterrence that requires genuine efforts toward disarmament and the rejection of all nuclear weapons strategies that do not meet rigid tests of morality.

It denounced all forms of war directed against civilian populations and was skeptical of the suggestion that any use of nuclear weapons can be kept within morally acceptable limits. It called for negotiations leading to disarmament and asked for improved international machinery to create an atmosphere of peace and justice. It reaffirmed opposition to abortion, which it found inconsistent with a recognition that there is a value to all human life.

Cardinal Bernardin greeted the bishops with an acknowledgment that "no person alive today has more powerfully called the Church to respond to the challenge of peace than Pope John Paul II." The Cardinal is an enthusiastic student of papal pronouncements. He was confident from the beginning that the pastoral letter would be in accord with the teachings of the Popes and the leadership of John Paul II.

In his opening address Cardinal Bernardin observed that publication of the third draft was followed by considerable commentary in the media about changes that were made. He explained the changes and the reasons for them. Here, in part, is how he explained extensive rewriting of the section on the moral theory of warfare: "Essentially we have stressed that the choices of 'just war' teaching or a 'nonviolent' position are options, available to individuals. Catholic teaching, however, traditionally and in this pastoral, is clear about the duty of the state to use force as a last resort, and the absolute need for state action to be assessed by moral criteria whenever force is used. In stating this case we have placed the just war criteria first, have expanded the explanation of them and have retained a distinct section on nonviolence. A particular concern of the third draft has been to show the relationship of these two dimensions of Catholic teaching and how they are to be understood in complementary fashion."

He explained that theologically the pastoral takes its direction from the Second Vatican Council's Pastoral

Constitution on the Church in the Modern World. He reminded the bishops that the need for prayer remains central: "We speak as a community of faith in this pastoral. We use the wisdom of philosophy and faith, the resources of science and politics, but all of these seem fragile before the danger of the age. They must be supplemented by the power of prayer for it is in prayer that our concluding paragraph (of the draft) takes on new meaning and provides continuing strength and hope: 'Behold I make all things new.'"

It was a radiant Cardinal Bernardin who said after the secret ballots had been counted that many religious denominations have shown support for the second and third drafts. Everything was over except rewriting the precis, or introductory summary, and incorporating the amendments into the text. Or was it just beginning? Bishop Fulcher was appointed to chair a committee of bishops to follow through on the pastoral, intended for use in countless parishes, classrooms and living rooms. Although opposition was quite limited, the bishops understood that a long educational program was ahead. Not all portions of the letter carry equal authority, the letter itself makes clear. It is possible to disagree and still be a good Catholic.

When Cardinal Bernardin was asked by reporters whether the Catholic Church had become a "peace church" he answered that the phrase has to be nuanced, that not everyone means the same thing when using it. "We have always been for peace," he told the reporters.

When he was asked about it he described the pastoral as "one of the most important initiatives taken by the Conference in a long time." Others, less restrained, called it the most significant and far-reaching public document ever

issued by the U.S. bishops. Many worked on it, and
perhaps no member of the staff worked harder than Father
Bryan Hehir, justice and peace specialist for the United
States Catholic Conference. Cardinal Bernardin received
between 5,000 and 6,000 letters.

Hundreds of editorials, columns and commentaries were
written. Bishops all over the country researched the document in each of its drafts and offered their comments.
There were heroic jobs of typing and retyping. The complete second, third and final drafts were published in
Origins and *The Chicago Catholic*, some hundred thou-
sand words altogether. But one man presided over the
development of the document, brought strong-minded
individuals together, ironed out problems, gained
widespread acceptance. No single name is affixed to the
final document, but his fellow bishops agree that Cardinal
Bernardin is the one who made it all turn out just right.

Perhaps some of those bishops and some of the journalists who told the world about the document shared
the feeling of James Kilcoyne, veteran photographer for
The Chicago Catholic, a man who has been at Cardinal
Bernardin's elbow and leaning over his shoulder in
Chicago parishes, Roman institutions and Cincinnati
offices. "When he touches you, you know you've been
touched. When he listens, you know you're being listened
to. He's a listening person and his mind seems to be as fast
as a computer."

"When I heard he was coming to Chicago I decided to
make the perfect photo, one that would tell all about
him," Jim Kilcoyne recalled. "I never made that photo.
Nobody can. There's too much to portray. I like to watch
his hands as he explains something. He always gives a sense

of action to his words. I've seen him give precious moments to listening. When he speaks he says the right thing. At the time of his first Christmas Eve Mass in the chapel of the Little Sisters of the Poor I was nearby when his mother, sitting in her wheelchair ready to take the figure of the baby Jesus to the altar, said that she hoped she'd do everything right. The Cardinal bent down, looked into her face and said, 'Honey, you always do everything right.'"

So maybe it is in the genes. In any event, nearly everyone agreed that Cardinal Bernardin had done things right in steering the complex pastoral letter along a sometimes bumpy road. Its adoption by a lopsided vote and the cheers it drew underscore the strength of the mind of Cardinal Bernardin.

Chapter Seventeen

THE final version of the pastoral letter on war and peace was hailed by religious leaders of many faiths. Words of encouragement and support were heard all over the country even before the revised document was printed.

Interfaith cooperation was not new to Cardinal Bernardin, a man who's always known where he stood and respected those who stand elsewhere in the religious community. He knows that the modern world includes millions of persons, some highly educated and some with little formal education, who believe in nothing they cannot see, touch, smell, taste or hear. These uncounted millions seem to be cut off from the reality of God's creation.

Not all who affirm God's presence act as though they really believe it. Arguments, sometimes violent, engage one Christian against another, one Moslem against another, one Jew or Hindu or Buddhist against another. Truth is elusive. Men and women benefit and suffer from their religious, cultural and national heritage.

From childhood Joseph Bernardin has looked for ways to draw people together, recognizing the good wherever he sees it without compromising his convictions as a Roman Catholic. Cardinal Newman, greatly respected by many who were not Roman Catholics, wrote that the Church "is for the many as well as for the few." He acknowledged that "the whole course of Christianity from the first, when we come to examine it, is but one series of troubles and disorders."

The Bernardin instinct is to try to make calm out of trouble and order out of disorder, understanding out of misunderstanding and unity out of confusion. That's one reason why he didn't hesitate to tackle the almost overwhelming issue of world peace and justice, and why so many respond cheerfully to those efforts.

The very month that the pastoral letter was adopted in Chicago the Governing Board of the National Council of Churches met in San Francisco, where it praised the pastoral. A board resolution hailed the condemnation of any first use of nuclear weapons and said: "We wholeheartedly join in the struggle to understand and respond to the challenge of peace for Christians so courageously carried forward by the National Conference of Catholic Bishops."

The previous December Cardinal Bernardin addressed the Protestant Foundation in Chicago's Marriott Hotel. "Protestant and Catholic," he said. "Those two words are pregnant with meaning." He continued. "Protestant. One thinks of Martin Luther declaring before the Diet of Worms on April 18, 1521: 'Here I stand, I cannot do otherwise.' Or Ralph Waldo Emerson writing about faith: 'It cannot be received second hand,' he said. 'Truly speaking it is not instruction but provocation, that I can receive from another soul. What he announces, I must find true in me, or reject; and on his word or his second, be he who he may, I can accept nothing. On the contrary, the absence of this primary faith is the presence of degradation.' The individual, committed to the Lord, striving to be true to his or her conscience in the midst of the stress and strain of life.

"And Catholic. The overtones of universality, reaching out to embrace all times, all places, all cultures, all classes. Taking seriously the magnanimity of Jesus reflected in his

beautiful image found in the Gospel according to John,
Chapter 14: 'In my Father's house there are many mansions. If there were not I would have told you, for I am going to make ready a place for you.' Catholicism embodies
that image of a large sprawling house containing an
immense family, united in the essentials of faith but not
always agreeing on all the implications of that faith; full of
energy and vitality, somehow resolving their spats before
they reach the point of fracture, striving to move together
as God's people living in an ecclesial community which
they see not so much as an institution as the living presence
of the Lord Jesus."

The Cardinal talked about the preparation of young
couples for marriage, preparation that includes a certain
amount of paperwork. The parish priest fills out a
questionnaire.

"Lately," Cardinal Bernardin told the Protestant Foundation, "some of our priests have noted that when they
come to the question which asks: 'What is your religion?'
some couples have responded, 'Christian.' The priest inquires further: 'Yes, but are you Catholic or Lutheran or
Methodist or Baptist or what? What specific kind of Christian are you?' In some cases, the response goes like this:
'Well, I was baptized Catholic (or Presbyterian or
whatever) but now I'm just a Christian. I found a group in
college that doesn't want to be encumbered with all that
baggage from the past. It seems to distract from what's
really important about God and religion. All those complicated doctrines and all those religious wars that were
fought in the name of Jesus. Who needs it? What I've
found is the simplicity of reading the Scriptures and
sharing together and praising the Lord by leading a good,
virtuous life.'"

Cardinal Bernardin observed that everybody can take some consolation from the fact that the spiritual dimension of life is important to the young. But he had another observation, that "the phenomenon I have just described carries a strong message of urgency to us who are leaders in the various churches, congregations and denominations. It urges us to look anew at our own respective traditions and to move forward at the same time with the work of ecumenism."

Another reaction is caution: "It is a caution couched in the old expression: 'He who does not learn from history is doomed to repeat it.' Sydney Ahlstrom's excellent work, *A Religious History of the American People*, is filled with many examples of individuals and groups who rejected their traditions in order to seek a pristine experience of the purity and simplicity of a religious community unencumbered by the baggage of the past. After a period of initial enthusiasm they encountered the challenges of the human condition. Issues of responsibility, authority, disagreements, finances, structure—all of these key realities of human existence had to be dealt with, together with the attendant frictions and stresses. I say this not as an older person seeking to pour cold water on the enthusiasm of young people, but as a fellow human being saying: 'Welcome to the club. We're all in this together.' We are the way we are not because we are bad people, but because we are human."

Using the sort of direct language often found in his public addresses, Cardinal Bernardin said that all history, including the history of Catholics and Protestants, is "a mixed bag." He listed some of the contents of that bag, saints and sinners, the generous and selfish, the beautiful and ugly, the corrupt and the manipulative. "But it goes beyond that," he said. "We belong to a very rich tradition which embodies the hard-earned wisdom of centuries of experience—an experience that can revitalize us today."

He recalled a visit to a religious book store, well stocked with records, wall plaques, candles, carved statues, inspirational literature, devotional reading, Bibles and Bible reference books.

"But there was not much challenging reading in the area of theology or ethics. I do not mention this in criticism of the store because I am sure the owners stocked items in which people were interested. And the place was doing a brisk business, a good sign that people thirst for religious nourishment. My concern is for a possible softening of the vigor of our intellectual tradition. True, some of our ancestors may have wasted time quibbling over matters that were quite peripheral to the faith. But we stand in mutual admiration of the intellectual accomplishments of such people as Augustine and Aquinas, Calvin and Luther, John Courtney Murray and Reinhold Niebur. We need to celebrate and renew that aspect of our separate and intertwined traditions."

He cited a need to study and evaluate bilateral consultations that have been in progress between the Roman Catholic Church and individual Protestant churches since the late Sixties. He said that the consultations "have sought to bring into clear focus the points that unite us and those that divide us, and to indicate those areas where there could be a greater convergence of positions."

He referred to a statement by Pope John Paul II and Anglican Archbishop Robert Runcie in June 1982: "(Our task) will be to continue the work already begun: to examine...the outstanding doctrinal differences which still separate us, with a view toward their eventual resolution; to study all that hinders the mutual recognition of the ministries of our communions; and to recommend what practical steps will be necessary when, on the basis of our unity in faith, we are able to proceed to the restoration of full communion. We are well aware that this. . .will not be easy, but we are encouraged by our reliance on the grace of God and by all that we have seen of the power of that grace in the ecumenical movement of our time.''

Cardinal Bernardin was concerned also about the tradition of service. What about the complexity of the world, so troubling to the young and so puzzling to all? ''What about the needs of all those suffering people? We have to resist the temptation to withdraw from it all and disengage ourselves,'' the Cardinal said.

''I know some folks who will not watch the evening newscast because it is all so depressing and, besides, 'What can one individual do about it?' One of the keystones of our tradition of service—both Catholic and Protestant—is based upon those words of Jesus which at first seem so ordinary but, on reflection, are so rich in meaning. In the Sixteenth Chapter of the Gospel according to Matthew he says: 'I am sending you out like sheep among wolves. So you must be wise like serpents and guileless like doves.' Those who have been most effective in responding to the needs of humanity have been men and women, Protestants and Catholics, who were able to negotiate those two apparently contradictory qualities. Guilelessness or simplicity of heart and wisdom or shrewdness—or as we sometimes hear around Chicago, 'street smarts.' It is precisely this tradition of service that takes us into the real world and prompts us to make moral judgments about what we see and experience. Some complain about this, but Jesus's contemporaries complained about him also when he addressed the issues of his day."

Cardinal Bernardin has been forthright in addressing major issues of the day, including some with interfaith implications. In major addresses to Jewish organizations he began with assurances of respect and friendship.

He told the National Jewish Community Relations Advisory Council in Cincinnati in 1979: "I come to you as a friend." In 1983 he said to the Chicago Board of Rabbis and the Jewish Federation of Metropolitan Chicago: "I come to you as your brother, Joseph." He told the Chicago groups that with reference to Israel Catholics and Jews "are united in many of our perspectives, but we also differ on some of them."

He said that Catholics and Jews want peace in the volatile Middle East. "I believe that Catholics generally support Israel and have positive attitudes toward it. Catholics relate sympathetically to Israel as a democracy in an increasingly totalitarian world. Moreover, Catholics are beginning to understand the religious and cultural factors which tie all Jews to the land of Israel."

The Cardinal cautioned that "some members of the Jewish community seem to be making the kind of support of Judaism and Israel found among certain evangelical groups the barometer for Jewish relations with mainline Christian churches, including the Catholic Church. This could create a problem for Catholic-Jewish relations. While Catholic theology has come to recognize clearly the permanence of the Jewish covenant, and while Catholics have grown in their appreciation of the Jewish land tradition as a result of Christian biblical scholarship, Israel will never play the kind of role in our theology that it does for some of the evangelical groups. Hence, while Catholics may retain a strong commitment to Israel, we cannot be expected to speak about this commitment in the same theological language as they.''

Cardinal Bernardin spoke plainly about unhappiness among Jews over a meeting between Pope John Paul II and Yasser Arafat, the Palestine Liberation Organization leader. ''The Catholic community generally sees such visits by the Holy Father as pastoral efforts at reconciliation. The Papacy has a tradition of talking with various world leaders.'' Meetings with leaders of the Soviet Union, Nicaragua, Poland, El Salvador and other countries ''in no way constitute an endorsement of their fundamental policies.'' He continued: ''Moreover, I have reason to believe that when the Pope did meet with Arafat he urged him to recognize Israel and to abandon terrorism.''

He talked frankly about ''many unjust practices, such as forced baptism,'' associated with Christian activities in the past. ''Today the Church is clearly committed to the principles of religious liberty, a commitment which of itself necessitates the rejection of all unfair proselytizing which might have taken place in the past.'' Christian witness, he explained, is to be distinguished from proselytism ''and is to be guided by the rules of justice and love.''

After addressing various Jewish concerns, he said that there also are Catholic concerns that call for dialogue and understanding.

''The first is aid to children who attend church-related schools. This has long been a sore spot among American Catholics, especially parents. I suggest that, in the spirit that has marked our dialogue in other areas, we now sit down together to discuss this topic. The anguish and hurt felt by Catholics at the systematic economic discrimination against them in their efforts to maintain what they consider their right to 'free' exercise of religion is very real and very deep.

"While there is still considerable opposition from the Jewish community, I am encouraged that some Jewish leaders have begun to call for a reassessment of the traditional line of opposition to any form of relief for parents who use their God-given and constitutional right to send their children to the school of their choice. I know, too, that the Union of Orthodox Jewish Congregations has dissented from the position of opposition assumed by other Jewish groups."

The Cardinal rejected the suggestion that the issue of respect for life, particularly relating to abortion, is sectarian. Acknowledging that the Catholic Church is more concerned about it than any other issue, abortion "is basically a question of human rights," he said, "the right of an unborn infant to live." He asked for more dialogue "so that we can avoid the misconceptions and stereotypes which plague us, so that we can develop greater understanding and sensitivity to deeply held convictions."

Cardinal Bernardin said that cooperation on social issues is encouraging and ought to be strengthened. He spoke of economic troubles, especially as they relate to the poor, and of racism. He invited his Jewish audience to join the Catholic bishops in their search for peace.

After he had finished speaking there was sustained applause. Rabbi Yechiel Eckstein, a national leader in interfaith cooperation, told me that the address was as powerful as he had expected from a spiritually powerful Catholic churchman.

Much of the world is prepared for the degree of understanding advocated by Cardinal Bernardin. "He's a gem," an Episcopal priest told me over lunch at the Chicago Press Club. Letters to the editor written by Methodists, Presbyterians, Jews, men and women of all faiths tell of their appreciation for his leadership. He presents an authentically ecumenical view that draws strength from the affirmation of his Roman Catholic foundations.

Chapter Eighteen

SOME of the young couples who visit rectories to talk about getting married are confused about the role of churches in the latter part of the Twentieth Century, as Cardinal Bernardin said in speaking to a Protestant group in Chicago.

It could be added that many Roman Catholics are confused about their own Church in a world that sometimes seems to act out its frustrations in one demonstration after another, demonstrations that continue for at least as long as television news cameras are pointed their way. Rules and regulations are a bother, although many of them are taken for granted to such an extent that when somebody violates them there can be painful consequences.

Americans generally accept the rules about stopping for red lights, driving on the right hand side of the road, paying sales taxes, placing stamps on letters before mailing them, endorsing checks before cashing them, dropping tokens or coins into bus fare boxes. They usually follow widely accepted customs, using knives and forks when they're dining out in steak houses, saying "goodbye" before hanging up telephones, restraining any urge to stand up and present a differing view after a homily has been delivered.

Most of us pass through the day observing rules and customs without much of a thought about them. But some rules are irksome to some of us; some just don't want to be bound by any regulations, although they probably wouldn't want to live in a community in which everybody shared that feeling.

When he was president of the National Conference of Catholic Bishops and the United States Catholic Conference, Archbishop Bernardin of Cincinnati talked about moral choices in society. "The subject of morality is the use and abuse of freedom," he wrote in an article for the National Catholic News Service. "Moral education is therefore education by which we grow in our ability to use freedom and to use it rightly."

He said that one approach to the subject "supposes that children, the first subjects of moral education, are so naturally good that they need only be left alone to do as they please in order to become morally good adults. Immorality comes from outside us; but if we were allowed to grow up following our natural inclinations, we would naturally do what is right. This would be true if human morality were no more complicated than animal behavior. In following their natural inclinations, animals spontaneously do what is right for them. But human beings are not simply animals, and human morality is a complex matter focused on freedom."

He observed that another approach "assumes that moral education consists simply in acquiring good habits through a process of conditioning based on rewards and punishments. Good habits are certainly desirable and should be encouraged. In fact, freely and deliberately acquired good habits are what we call virtues. But purely automatic actions which result from imposed conditioning are not free acts. So, although conditioning is suited to training animals, it is not appropriate to the moral education of human beings learning to make good use of their freedom."

Again and again in his public statements, Cardinal Bernardin has urged freedom and a correct understanding of how to achieve it. "Moral education is an aspect of socialization—the process by which we grow in our ability to assume roles and responsibilities as members of communities," he wrote. "One problem for moral education today is a tendency to overemphasize individual, isolated self-fulfillment apart from fulfillment in and through communal obligations. By contrast, a sound system of moral education places individuals in their social context and encourages them to assume their obligations not only to themselves but to others."

This is supported, he said, by the moral teaching of Jesus Christ, which has been described as a "law of love." He alluded to St. Augustine's famous words: "Love God, and then do what you will." This, he emphasized, "does not mean that one who loves God can do absolutely anything, confident that whatever he or she does will be morally right. It means instead that, to the extent one loves God (and therefore also loves one's neighbor, which is the second great commandment laid down by Christ), one will do everything which love of God and neighbor requires and will avoid doing whatever is incompatible with such love."

Learning how to discern Christ's moral teaching is an essential part of developing a sense of Christian family and community life. Catholics look to the Bible, prayer, human experience and even human history. In a special way they look to the Church. Cardinal Bernardin explained this with a quotation from the documents of the Second Vatican Council: "In the formation of their consciences, the Christian faithful ought carefully to attend to the sacred and certain doctrine of the Church."

He said that when the Church does "propose moral norms and standards of behavior in Christ's name, as it has often done and will continue to do, its teaching is authoritative and trustworthy. This follows from Christ's promise to send his Spirit to the Church and remain with it for all time. And, because Christ confers a special teaching office on bishops in union with the Pope, the moral teaching of the bishops united with the Holy Father has unique weight and credibility."

Cardinal Bernardin has read the articles and the poll results. Much more important than that, he has shared countless pastoral hours with individuals in trouble. He knows that developing a sound moral foundation and living in accord with it is the work of a lifetime. He knows that there are many temptations to shrug off moral concerns in the name of misguided personal freedom. Cardinal Bernardin knows that sexual problems can cause anxiety, remorse, even the repudiation of personal obligations.

He talked about this in a 1980 intervention at the World Synod of Bishops, mentioning "the existence of a significant gap" between Church teaching on sexual morality "and the ideas and attitudes on the same subject held by many of the laity and even many priests." He referred to two needs: "The first concerns our manner of conceptualizing and presenting our teaching on sexuality and the ethical and moral norms which flow from that teaching. The second has to do more with motivation—with helping people not only to understand the teaching more fully but to respond to it in an affirmative way."

He emphasized four points: "Sexuality is a gift from God. Therefore, it is good in itself and, used as God intends, enriching and ennobling. This point must be stressed so as to counteract dualistic thinking of the past and also of the present which denigrates the body and sexuality. Sexuality is a relational power. It is not merely a capacity for performing specific acts. It is part of our God-given natural power or capacity for relating to others. It colors the qualities of sensitivity, warmth, openness and mutual respect in our interpersonal relationships.

"In this connection, it is important to note that human sexuality also has a social dimension. As a constituent part of our nature, it influences our societal relationships and well-being, as well as our personal relationships with other individuals. Understood in this way, sexuality cannot be equated with genitality, which is a narrower concept referring to the physical expressions of sexuality leading to genital union. The special context of marriage is needed for the supreme physical expression of sexuality to serve human love and life generously and without the deception that premarital and extramarital relations contain."

He said that it cannot be assumed that people understand and accept a natural law ethic, although the natural law tradition should not be abandoned. It can be enriched, he said, in working toward "a more holistic approach to sexuality and conjugal love."

In that Synod intervention he quoted Pope John Paul II, who said in a Washington Mall homily that "in order that Christian marriage may favor the total good and development of the married couple it must be inspired by the Gospel, and thus be open to new life...new life to be given and accepted generously." The Bernardin intervention spoke of "the incompleteness and therefore the basic disorder of masturbation, premarital sex and homosexual acts."

In a 1977 talk at a Knights of Columbus convention in Indianapolis, the future Archbishop of Chicago touched on the question of human rights and morality. He insisted that human rights consideration have an important place in United States foreign and domestic policies.

Abortion, he said, "is a crucial test for our respect for the right to life." He told the Knights: "Our concern for abortion as a preeminent violation of the fundamental right to life should make us sensitive to other violations, or threatened violations, of this right. There is dismaying evidence that disrespect for life extends not only to the unborn but, at the other end of life's spectrum, to the aged and infirm.

"The deprivation and neglect in which many elderly persons in this country live is a standing indictment of the moral insensitivity of our society." He warned of abuses of the rights of the handicapped and the poor. "One is aware in our time of a frightening and morally obtuse tendency to think and speak in terms of inferior lives, unwanted lives, lives subject to being demeaned and even destroyed because, in the estimate of some, to reverence and sustain them is too costly or simply too inconvenient for the rest of us."

The years following Vatican Council II have brought an increased sense of personal responsibility to countless Catholics. When some of the rules were relaxed or done away with there was a feeling that possibly none of the rules had lasting validity.

There was a feeling that each person ought to be a theologian, moralist, Bible scholar and specialist in half a dozen other fields that each calls for a lifetime of preparation and practice.

There were some who put abstaining from meat on

Fridays on the same moral level as abstaining from the destruction of human life through abortion. If one rule no longer applied, why bother about the other? That confusion may explain Cardinal Bernardin's call for deeper intellectual roots to support the tree of spiritual understanding.

Chapter Nineteen

NOT every member of the clergy is at home with the laity. Catholic priests and Protestant ministers spend a lot of time attending clergy meetings and have powerful ties with seminary classmates. Priests often live together in rectories. Golfing partners are likely to be clerical. Priests frequently vacation together. There are no wives or children in the dining room.

But priests provide ministerial service to the laity much more often than they do to each other, and lots of priests spend free time with members of their own families.

Cardinal Bernardin is close to his family, not only in the United States but in Italy. His friends include lay women and men. He's able to understand the anxieties of parents and children, the pressures that squeeze so much out of the poor, the devastation that can come to a family through illness, the satisfactions of life at home.

When he was Father Bernardin in Charleston, not long after he'd been ordained a priest, one of his friends was Father Louis Sterker, originally from Brooklyn but by then a priest in South Carolina. He became Monsignor Sterker and later a pastor in Columbia; but long before that he took young Father Bernardin along for a visit at the Mosimann home. Father Sterker knew of the young priest's interest in music. Mrs. Mosimann was choir director at the Charleston cathedral and everyone in the family was an opera buff. The diocese covered a lot of territory, but the Catholic share of the total population was less than 1 percent. About 14,000 Catholics lived in Charleston.

One of the Mosimann sisters, Octavie, went to work for

Father Bernardin. He was chancellor, secretary to Bishop John J. Russell, head of Catholic Charities, chaplain at a military school and wearer, altogether, of perhaps half a dozen hats. Miss Mosimann worked as his secretary in the afternoons and for another priest in the mornings.

Then in 1958 Bishop Russell moved to Richmond and Paul J. Hallinan became the Bishop of Charleston. That's when Octavie Mosimann became secretary to both Father Bernardin and Bishop Hallinan, "four of my best years," she recalled later. "They worked together so well." They were to work together again in a different setting, when Bishop Hallinan became the Archbishop of Atlanta and Father Bernardin became his auxiliary bishop. "Everybody who knew him when he was a young priest felt that someday he might become a bishop. I never thought that he'd become the Archbishop of Chicago and that I'd still be his secretary."

Archbishop Hallinan, an influential and beloved figure in the Church, died in March of 1968. On April 10 of that year Bishop Bernardin was appointed general secretary in Washington. Although she'd worked for him for a decade in Charleston, Miss Mosimann did not accompany Bishop Bernardin to Atlanta. She knew the city, though, and before she accepted the Chancery job in Charleston she told her new employer that she'd have to be given vacation time once a year at the time of Opera Week in Atlanta.

She cheerfully accepted Bishop Bernardin's invitation to be his secretary when he went to Washington. Two of her sisters and two brothers lived in the Washington area, all of them married, providing Miss Mosimann an abundance of nieces and nephews. Opera Week, though, lost out when Miss Mosimann became the first woman admitted to meetings of the bishops, meetings that coincided with the annual Atlanta week of music.

A secretary's insights confirm what much of the world knows about Cardinal Bernardin. After working for him during his four years in Washington and his ten years in Cincinnati, then accompanying him to Chicago, she knew his ways and thought they were pretty good. Even when he was a young priest, she recalled years afterward, he often typed his homilies. "The reason he reads his homilies and his public talks is that he's so particular about what he says. He has thought it all out and written it carefully, just as he wants to say it."

Cardinal Bernardin still does much of his own typing. He likes to use razor tip felt pens for writing in longhand on legal pads similar to those used many years ago by Archbishop Hallinan.

Cardinal Bernardin has never accepted division in his office, Miss Mosimann told me. "He sets an atmosphere of harmony that prevails in his office and even in committees. He's a considerate employer and he's much more disciplined than I am. He has tremendous energy and the ability to move from one subject to another. I think it's a fantastic trait to be able to work on one thing, then accept an interruption in the form of a telephone call and show no irritation. He has to be firm, but he is very human. He is concerned about people. He has a quality that is much more than control. He really does not get angry, even when he is provoked." Not every bishop, government official or business executive can count on that sort of appraisal from observant secretaries.

Everyone close to him develops the same respect for his decency, his interest in others, his judgments and his

willingness to work hard. Father James Roache, his
administrative assistant in Chicago, came to know him
well during the Synod of Bishops in 1974 when they both
lived in Rome's Villa Stritch.

"My early impressions of him, which I formed when
I was one of two press officers for the bishops in
Washington, were reenforced in Rome," Father Roache
told me in Chicago. "He never tried to skirt an issue; he
always found a way to deal with issues with clarity. He's
spent a couple of years chairing the pastoral letter committee; if another one or six or dozen challenges come his way
he's likely to say yes to any of them. He has a great ability
to compartmentalize work. He can keep issues separate
and clear. He's able to do one thing at a time and to apply
a lot of energy to the doing. He has his heart in each thing
that he does. He's empathetic. He can appreciate the
frustration or the joy of others."

Father Roache said he's very comfortable living with
Cardinal Bernardin in his official residence in Chicago.
"He enjoys visiting, chatting, eating at home. He puts
everyone at ease. He creates a home environment."

I commented that a few weeks earlier I'd asked the Cardinal to give me some information for a news story. He
began speaking about the issue in the language of journalism, virtually dictating a story that would have been acceptable to *The New York Times*. I asked Father Roache
whether there's anything that the Cardinal doesn't do well.
He answered: "Golf."

But he went on to say that the Cardinal has a gift for
editing. "Clarity is his big thing. He sees that communication should be clear. He will not put off getting at the heart
of an issue. If he disagrees with someone he will quickly

acknowledge a difference. He seems to be saying, 'Here's where I am; I respect where you are.' He's comfortable about delegating work that must be done. It is clear that he wants subsidiarity. Problems that can be handled by a department head should be.

"To all of this he adds a spiritual dimension. He wants his staff to know that we're not running a bank or an airline, but that we're serving a church."

Father Roache found that his own life had become both busier and more fulfilling. He sees Cardinal Bernardin as a bishop, pastor, witness, preacher. He tries to help remove some of the necessary detail, helping the Cardinal to have more time for the important things that he alone can do. "He's a good mentor," Father Roache said. "His quality of dealing with many issues with frankness offers a great learning opportunity. His spirituality is transparent and disciplined.

"He will be measured eventually in terms of the great church leaders of this century and the next. He has a visionary commitment to make the Gospel come alive in the real world. He can deal honestly and sympathetically with groups, encouraging them to make the Beatitudes a part of their Christian living."

Father Roache agrees with others who see Cardinal Bernardin's love for the Church expressing itself in the development of leadership across the board, among clergy and religious and laity. I said that I thought this would encourage increased vocations to the priesthood, because young men will see in Cardinal Bernardin an authentic model for Christian service.

Father Roache nodded his agreement: "Families will be proud to have sons become like him. Parish priests will be glad to encourage vocations. The Cardinal preaches the gospel of vocations to the clergy, pointing out that we owe this to the future. He gives high priority to anything that relates to seminaries or seminarians and he encourages the work of the Serra Club."

Cardinal Bernardin has relatively few times of absolute privacy. That may be why he likes to drive his own car to some of the many places he visits in the course of a week.

Father Roache put it this way: "He's extremely generous. He does not hoard his time. He is not a workaholic, as some say, but he wants to respond to others and to needs wherever he sees them. He's an avid reader. He works his way through three newspapers before breakfast. He enjoys research and writing and he's at work on major documents concerning Christology and liturgy. He always has time for his mother. He visits her daily whenever possible. He remembers people and he remembers his roots. He's sensitive to people."

Father Roache began his assignment as administrative assistant in what had been a conference room, separated from the Cardinal's office only by Miss Mosimann's office. On the other side of the Archbishop's office sits another priest whose respect for Cardinal Bernardin's accomplishments grows daily. Father John R. Keating, chancellor and vicar general, was Administrator of the Archdiocese during the weeks following Cardinal Cody's death. His closest friends call him Dick (and only a handful of close friends call Miss Mosimann Tanchie.)

Father Keating's first observation of Cardinal Bernardin in action was identical to that of many others: "One of his obvious strengths is that he puts people at ease. He is able to neutralize tension and apprehension without apparently trying. There are no awkward moments with him. His personality somehow obviates awkwardness."

Father Keating lived in the official residence of Chicago's archbishops during his term as Administrator. On a Friday, the day before it was announced that the Archbishop of Cincinnati would move to Chicago, Father Keating was meeting with the Clergy Personnel Board at the residence when he was called to the phone. Archbishop Pio Laghi, the Apostolic Delegate, was on the line to say that an announcement would be made the next morning. "It will be Bernardin," Archbishop Laghi confided, adding that nothing could be disclosed before the official announcement was made.

"I returned to the board meeting," Father Keating said later. "The members were speculating on the name of the next archbishop. I had to go to supper with them that night, and the conversation was all about who the next archbishop would be." He resisted the temptation to drop a blockbuster into the conversation.

The new Ordinary was in Rome when the announcement was made. He tried to reach Father Keating by phone Saturday night, after he returned to Cincinnati, but didn't get through until Sunday morning. "Later he called to say that he was coming to Chicago for one day," Father Keating said. "I had to prepare his itinerary, and that's when I became a little nervous. He wanted to visit Mount Carmel Cemetery, where Cardinal Cody was interred; he wanted to visit the cathedral, which he'd seen before; he wanted to visit the Chancery and the seminary at Mundelein. We went to Mundelein on the day of the clergy golf tournament. Archbishop Bernardin happened to have a golf shirt with him and he put it on. We went to the eleventh tee where hot dogs were being served and watched a few of the players hit off. We knew they were trying their best, but their nervousness was shown by errant shots."

Father Keating handled many of the introductions, and was impressed by the thoroughness of Archbishop Bernardin's homework. He required little briefing.

After he returned to Cincinnati he was sent reports on the administration of the Archdiocese, which Father Keating felt he accepted without criticism. "He never seemed inquisitive. He accepted things as they were, and that put all of us at ease. He gave the impression that he had confidence in us and in what we were doing. What impressed me the most was his marvelous mind, which always seems to be working. He's always seeking the best way to handle an issue. I thought about the time back in seminary days when I was studying Thomistic philosophy and recalled the capacity of the human mind to fold back on itself, what's called "double reflection," reflecting on one's own thinking. During the first week that Bernardin was here I saw that he had a tremendous capacity for double reflection.

"His instructions to me were simple: 'Whatever you're doing, keep doing it.' He makes many decisions, but everybody here is at ease with him. He does not foment tensions. We all enjoy having him here in his office. I can see how many visitors he has and I can see that he's extremely punctual. He's organized and gracious. He has all the right traits in abundance. He's quick to grasp the complexities of a situation. Some of his ability in that respect shows in his penchant for phrases such as 'on the other hand.' Somebody quipped that his coat of arms should carry the words 'On the other hand.' One of his favorite words is 'nevertheless.' All of this shows his capacity to consider all sides of a question in order to understand it. He has a quaint combination of a penetrating mind and a playful sense of humor, a sense of light humor.''

So three of those who work most closely with Cardinal Bernardin, in offices that connect with his in the Archdiocesan Pastoral Center, recognize the same qualities of incisiveness, energy, thoughtfulness and prayerfulness. These are among the basic ingredients of the mind of Cardinal Bernardin.

The same qualities are seen by clergy and laity, men and women. He does not skirt issues and he seldom makes enemies in the course of being direct. Back in 1975, when he was president of the National Conference of Catholic Bishops, he issued a statement affirming the Catholic Church's teaching that "women are not to be ordained to the priesthood.''

He explained: "It is not correct to say that no serious theological obstacle stands in the way of ordaining women to the priesthood, and the fact that women have not been ordained up to now can be explained simply by culturally conditioned notions of male superiority. There is a serious theological issue. Throughout its history the Catholic Church has not called women to the priesthood. Although many of the arguments presented in times gone by on this subject may not be defensible today, there are compelling reasons for this practice.''

For some reason interviewers return over and over to that question, one that Cardinal Bernardin was being asked after he moved to Chicago. His answers are always the same in substance. Yet those answers have not caused the kind of rift that some might have expected, because

Cardinal Bernardin's frankness and his devotion to the Church are equally respected. His high opinion of women is so plainly evident that the issue cannot be confused. Neither can his own respect for the laity, women and men. He reminded the Archdiocesan Council of Catholic Women during a 1982 Chicago luncheon that the Second Vatican Council "stated explicitly that the laity's specific role is to bring the message of the Gospel to the world."

He declared at that time that "God wills all women and men to participate and share in his divine life and being." Because he believes what he says, his listeners pay close attention. He says again and again that the presence of the risen Lord among men and women is a challenge to each person to live according to the vision offered the world by Jesus.

Chapter Twenty

YOU'VE probably had one in your family, a little boy who found out how to take a clock apart. If he was a bright fellow he was able to put it back together and make it run better than before. Anybody can complain about a clock that doesn't keep time. Not everybody can fix it. Throughout the Catholic Church Cardinal Bernardin is admired as one who can make things work, who can even, to borrow an inadequate analogy, make the Church run on time.

He was a young man when be became chancellor of the Diocese of Charleston. During fourteen years, serving under four bishops, he held such additional assignments as vicar general, diocesan consultor and administrator of the diocese during a time when the See was vacant. He was born in Columbia, South Carolina, on April 2, 1928 to Joseph and Maria M. Simion Bernardin.

After he left the University of South Carolina he studied at St. Mary's College in Kentucky, then went to St. Mary's University and Seminary, operated by the Sulpicians in Baltimore. There he received an A.B. degree in philosophy before going to the Catholic University of America in Washington where he received a master's degree in education in 1952.

By December 1959 he was known as Msgr. Bernardin. On March 9, 1966 Pope Paul VI appointed him to Atlanta as auxiliary bishop. His friend and mentor, Archbishop Hallinan, was the principal consecrator when Msgr. Bernardin was ordained a bishop in Charleston's Cathedral of St. John the Baptist. In Atlanta he became vicar general

193

and rector of the Cathedral of Christ the King. After Archbishop Hallinan died in March of 1968 Bishop Bernardin
became Administrator of the Archdiocese of Atlanta. On
April 10 of that year he was elected general secretary of the
National Conference of Catholic Bishops, which was
created in response to the Second Vatican Council's call
for national organizations of the hierarchy, and of the
United States Catholic Conference, which succeeded the
National Catholic Welfare Conference as the permanent
secretariat of the U.S. bishops

During all of those years he was honing his organizational skills, which 'e applied energetically to the
reorganization of the episcopal conference. He told a
Chicago group long afterward that he spent a couple of
years implementing an elaborate plan of reorganization
and then a couple of years deimplementing it.

In fact, he put the plan into effect and then, as a compe-
tent administrator, adapted it to meet conditions that the
planners had not anticipated. That ability to adapt is rare
in the bureaucratic world. It is almost priceless in a leader
of perhaps the world's oldest bureaucractic system.

By the time he departed, an effective administrative
apparatus had been put in place at 1312 Massachusetts
Avenue, N.W., in the national capital. When he left
Washington in the fall of 1972 to become the Archbishop
of Cincinnati he recalled some of his work during the
previous five years. He declined to talk about "his" accomplishments or "his" contributions. Instead he talked
about what "the Conference" had done to develop itself
and to support the life of the Church throughout the
country.

In an interview with Jerry Filteau of the National
Catholic News Service, Bishop Bernardin said that the

Conference "is not a 'super-Church.'" He said that the "actual implementation of decisions made by bishops as members of the episcopal conference takes place at the local level. At the same time, no one will deny the influence of the episcopal conference on the life of the Church in this country." He reflected on that influence, remarking that it touched on liturgy, ecumenism, priestly formation and the permanent diaconate. He said that opening the meetings of the bishops to the media "has taken away some of the mystery, and perhaps now the vision of the Conference that some people have is more in line with the reality that has always existed."

He said that immediately after the Vatican Council there was a feeling of excitement and there was "a certain novelty about some of the things that needed to be done," creating "a great deal of anticipation." But, he said, "We've now moved into another phase—more important than the first, perhaps, if not as exciting. Our task now is to test some of the implications of the Council in the light of our pastoral experience. This work is not always glamorous, and it necessarily involves much study and time."

Study and time. From boyhood Joseph Bernardin has applied himself to study, in order to get at the heart of a situation, and then has applied his time efficiently in order to get results. His most important time is the time he spends in prayer. Spiritual considerations always head his personal agenda. He took that agenda with him to the Archdiocese of Cincinnati, where there were 529,000 Catholics in a total population of 2,670,000. He also took much that he had learned in Washington, drawing upon that experience to improve the organizational structure in Cincinnati.

As one who was present for his installation by Archbishop Luigi Raimondi, then the Apostolic Delegate and later to become Cardinal Raimondi, I felt the enthusiasm of Cincinnati Catholics who already knew a great deal about their new Ordinary. That was December 19, 1972.

Pope John Paul II appointed Archbishop Bernardin to Chicago on July 10, 1982 and he was installed at Holy Name Cathedral on August 25 by Archbishop Laghi. This time he moved to an archdiocese with 2,374,000 Catholics who were part of a total population of 5,690,000. Again he faced concerns of organization and reorganization. Again he applied study and time to the issues.

He knew that it would be good to increase the number of auxiliary bishops, but he needed time and study. He knew that something had to be done to reverse the annual operating deficits, to address the requirements of a large Hispanic community, to encourage a substantial black Catholic community, to stimulate vocations to Church service and to strengthen the sense of Christian sharing among many groups. There were discords to be healed and disagreements to be set aside. Cardinal Bernardin seemed to be everywhere, to talk with everyone. He wanted to get at the facts, but he wanted everyone to perceive as he did that a powerful spiritual commitment provides the only realistic foundation for the Church.

He moved quickly to dispel anxiety about the handling of finances, which had grown out of newspaper reports that his predecessor may have been too informal on one hand and too private on the other hand in administering the Archdiocese.

He appointed an Audit Committee comprised of outstanding community leaders of established business integrity. He instituted a system of financial reporting that corresponded to guidelines developed by the National Conference of Catholic Bishops, one that's intended to provide greater consistency in diocesan financial reporting. He explained this in a pastoral letter, published December 17, 1982 in *The Chicago Catholic*.

His reputation for not skirting difficult issues was sustained in that letter, in which he said that he wanted to "report the efforts that have been made to review certain questions which had arisen about the late John Cardinal Cody's administration. The inquiry begun by the federal government in November 1980 was formally closed in July of this year with a public announcement that the institution of an investigation does not indicate that any wrongdoing has in fact occurred. As the Cardinal's successor, I felt it my responsibility to make a personal inquiry so that whatever lingering doubts might exist could be cleared up as quickly and completely as possible."

The pastoral letter continued: "Even before the Cardinal's death a diligent effort had been made to obtain every personal financial record relevant to his seventeen-year tenure. On the basis of an inquiry made by the attorneys and accountants, the records collected, information obtained from interviews and estimates made when records were not available, it has been estimated that the Cardinal had spendable personal receipts of approximately $38,000 per year. (The sources of these funds were salary and investment income and the gifts he received; in later years, Social Security payments were an additional source.) Moreover, the available data indicate that his total personal expenditures did not exceed the total estimated personal receipts."

The letter explained: "I have also been advised that Cardinal Cody did not always follow preferred accounting procedures. This resulted in some confusion in the records. I believe such departures were the result of a failure to attend to detail and the pressing demands of an extraordinarily busy schedule. I now bring the matter to a close."

In his pastoral letter, Archbishop Bernardin said that he had closed the contingency fund account. "Every account maintained by the Archdiocese will hereafter be subject to strict auditing procedures," he wrote. "I ask all members of the Archdiocese to remember Cardinal Cody for the more than fifty years he served the Church and for the good he accomplished during his seventeen years in Chicago."

That's the way Cardinal Bernardin remembered his predecessor when he delivered the homily on the first anniversary of Cardinal Cody's death: "The Cardinal's years here in Chicago coincided with an interesting and exciting, but also difficult time: the post-conciliar period during which many significant changes took place in our Church as well as in society generally. Despite the fact that his background and training were of another era and another mentality, Cardinal Cody did all he could to implement the teaching of the Second Vatican Council. The difficulties he encountered stemmed, for the most part, from his strong convictions about how the Church should be governed in an age when the expectations and aspirations of people are so different from what they were in earlier times.

"The Cardinal accomplished a great deal in his seventeen years. We all benefit today from so many of his initiatives. Despite criticism and illness, he never gave up; to the end he was determined to serve the Church as best he could." There were smiles when Cardinal Bernardin said "As Cardinal Cody's successor, I probably am more aware than anyone else of the ecstasy and the agony of being the Archbishop of Chicago.''

Cardinal Bernardin told the Holy Name Cathedral congregation: ''I am sure, of course, that there are times when he must smile as he sees what I am trying to do. I can hear him: 'A bright idea, Joe; I'll give you ''A'' for effort, but if you only knew what I know!' And when I think he might be saying that, I respond: 'I know, John, but let me enjoy the freedom of not knowing any better; let me enjoy it before I learn too much!' ''

Cardinal Bernardin, the spiritual leader and temporal organizer, said in a homily just one day before that: ''There is a fundamental unity in the Church because its founder and its head is Jesus, the Lord—the only Lord—who has redeemed us and who accompanies us each day on our earthly pilgrimage.'' He said a moment later: ''But there is also a marvelous diversity in the Church.'' He compared the Church to a mosaic composed of many different pieces, each reflecting a different shape and color. Within a month there was evidence of that diversity while Cardinal Bernardin gave a Pentecost homily in the same cathedral. Across the street there were demonstrators holding signs and placards, pro-lifers supporting Pope John Paul II and others supporting Agnes Mary Mansour, who quit the Sisters of Mercy rather than give up her job as social services director for the State of Michigan. The Holy See reportedly urged her to resign from the state post, where her responsibilities included handling Medicaid abortion funding. The Second Vatican Council called abortion and infanticide ''abominable crimes,'' but some of Ms. Mansour's supporters saw the issue as one relating to ''due process'' and conscience. Cardinal Bernardin's homily, prepared before the demonstrators appeared, focused attention on the Holy Spirit and "his powerful presence among us." The Cardinal spoke of the Holy Spirit's role in promoting peace.

"Unfortunately, the human family has not enjoyed much peace in recent years," the Cardinal said. "Tensions and conflicts abound everywhere: Central America, the Middle East, Northern Ireland, Poland and many other places." He said that tensions and hostilities could be observed in the United States, in Chicago itself, and he said that they undermine the common good.

His search for ways to establish the common good is evident throughout Cardinal Bernardin's ministry. That search has taken him to many places. In 1977 it took him to the White House, where he and five other bishops spent an hour with President Carter. The President at that time reaffirmed his opposition to abortion and to government policies that encourage it. A year before Bernardin was one of five bishops who met with President Ford to talk about the resettlement of Southeast Asia refugees, abortion, the need for more food in developing nations, the agony of an estimated ten or twelve million illegal aliens and the unfairness of financial discrimination against children who attend nonpublic schools.

In 1977 he publicly deplored, on behalf of all of the U.S. bishops, the "repression of black leadership in South Africa and the banning of those white men whose voices were raised on the side of justice." He works vigorously to overcome every kind of racial and religious discrimination and to establish peace where there is fighting.

To accomplish that he draws upon rich spiritual resources. Anyone who doubts the efficacy of prayer might benefit from taking a close look at the Cardinal and his life. To accomplish order in other ways he draws upon his remarkable experience as an administrator and leader. Only he and Archbishop Kelly of Louisville, among all of the bishops of the country, have served as general secretary of the episcopal conference, supervising the work of hundreds and the activities of a number of specialized agencies, relating to government at the highest levels and working closely with the Holy See.

Much of what Cardinal Bernardin achieved during his Washington years was felt in Chicago, when he set about reorganizing the leadership of the Archdiocese. Characteristically, he created a committee of particularly qualified individuals, told the committee what he wanted to have accomplished and then turned the committee loose to do the job. Out of that came a major restructuring of the Archdiocesan Pastoral Center, headquarters for some sixty agencies and offices.

Bishop Daniel P. Reilly of Norwich, Connecticut, a member of the committee charged with drafting the collective pastoral letter on war and peace, visited the Archbishop's residence in Chicago not long after it became the Bernardin home. He told a Chicago priest, who wondered what sort of man had become his Archbishop: "You're going to marvel at his marvelous mind."

It is a mind nurtured by prayer, recalling the recommendation made by St. Paul to the Philippians: "Your attitude must be that of Christ." That's how it appears in the New American Bible. The King James Version puts it in different words: "Let this mind be in you, which was also in Christ Jesus." The model for thinkers is also the model for doers. The model chosen decades ago by a young Joe Bernardin explains much that is remarkable about the mind of today's Cardinal.

A Cardinal-Watcher's Datebook

April 2, 1928. Joseph Louis Bernardin born to Joseph and Maria M. Bernardin, Italian immigrants, in Columbia, South Carolina.

1948. Received a bachelor of philosophy degree from St. Mary's Seminary in Baltimore, following studies at the University of South Carolina and St. Mary's College, St. Mary, Kentucky.

1952. Awarded a master's degree in education at the Catholic University of America in Washington.

April 26, 1952. Ordained to the priesthood by Bishop John J. Russell in Columbia, South Carolina, for the Diocese of Charleston.

1954-1956. Vice chancellor of the Diocese of Charleston.

1956-1966. Chancellor of the Diocese of Charleston.

1962-1966. Vicar general, diocesan consultor.

March 9, 1966. Appointed auxiliary bishop in Atlanta.

April 26, 1966. Ordained titular bishop of Lugura and auxiliary bishop of Atlanta.

1966-1968. Pastor of Christ the King Cathedral in Atlanta.

1968-1972. First general secretary of the National Conference of Catholic Bishops and the United States Catholic Conference, with headquarters in Washington.

1970-1972. Member of the Pontifical Commission for Social Communications.

November 21, 1972. Appointed Archbishop of Cincinnati.

December 19, 1972. Installed as Archbishop of Cincinnati at St. Peter in Chains Cathedral.

1973. Appointed to the Sacred Congregation of Bishops and elected one of four United States delegates to the World Synod of Bishops.

May 1973 to December 1981. Member of Board of Trustees of the Catholic University of America. Elected again for 1983-1984 academic year.

1974. Elected to the permanent council of the World Synod of Bishops.

1974-1977. President of the National Conference of Catholic Bishops and the United States Catholic Conference.

1974. Voted "top personality" in a poll of Catholic editors in the United States.

1975. Issued a pastoral letter to priests on the Eucharist.

1975. Cited by Hebrew Union College in Cincinnati for his efforts to create "a spirit of cooperation and understanding between Catholics and Jews."

1975. Member of the American Revolution Bicentennial Advisory Committee and the President's Advisory Commission on Refugees.

1976. Visited Poland for ten days at the invitation of Stefan Cardinal Wyszynski for the rededication of the United States to Mary at Our Lady of Czestochowa Shrine.

1976. "Most influential religious leader" in a poll of key Americans by U.S. News & World Report.

April 26, 1977. Twenty-fifth anniversary of ordination to the priesthood and eleventh anniversary of ordination as a bishop.

1977. Traveled to Hungary.

1978. Named chairman of the board, National Catholic Educational Association.